A PASSION FOR BOOKS

A Passion for Books

Edited by

Dale Salwak

Professor of English
Citrus College
California

St. Martin's Press
New York

A PASSION FOR BOOKS

St. Martin's Press, Scholarly and Reference Division,
175 Fifth Avenue, New York, N.Y. 10010

First published in the United States of America in 1999

This book is printed on paper suitable for recycling and
made from fully managed and sustained forest sources.

Printed in Great Britain

ISBN 0–312–21884–2

Library of Congress Cataloging-in-Publication Data
A passion for books / edited by Dale Salwak.
p.   cm.
Includes bibliographical references (p.   ) and index.
ISBN 0–312–21884–2 (alk . paper)
1. Books and reading—United States.   2. Books and reading—Great
Britain.   3. Critics—United States—Books and reading.   4. Critics-
–Great Britain—Books and reading.   5. Authors, English—Books and
reading.   I. Salwak, Dale.
Z1003.2.P37   1998
028—dc21   98–34147
                                                                 CIP

Myrtle C. Bachelder
In memoriam
1908–97

Contents

Preface

'People find the books they need,' writes Lance Morrow: 'to escape, to edify and impress, to keep sane, to touch other intelligences, to absorb a little grace.' For the obsessive reader, the book-possessed, Flaubert said, reading is life. It isn't, of course, but we know what he means.

Eudora Welty, for example, says in *One Writer's Beginnings* that she is unable to 'remember a time when I was not in love with them – with the books themselves, cover and binding and the paper they were printed on, with their smell and their weight and with their possessions in my arms, captured and carried off to myself.' Lynne Sharon Schwartz, another early reader, says in *Ruined by Reading* that the act changed her life, starting 'innocently enough,' but then 'it infiltrated. It didn't replace living; it infused it, till the two became inextricable, like molecules of hydrogen and oxygen in a bead of water.' And Anatole Broyard recalls of his life in the Greenwich Village scene that 'it was as if we didn't know where we ended and books began. Books were our weather, our environment, our clothing. We didn't simply read books; we became them. We took them into ourselves and made them into our histories . . . Books gave us balance . . . Books steadied us . . . They gave us gravity.'

It is in this spirit that three years ago I invited eighteen prominent individuals to reflect from varying perspectives (as novelist, scholar, collector, editor, performer or publisher) upon the value and importance of books in their lives. I wanted to create an anthology that would capture for some and rekindle for others the fascination, the enlightenment, and the sheer joy that books can give to the willing. I also wanted to offer, in a modest way, a defense against the many gloomy voices in our so-called electronic age that say the printed book as we know it will soon be obsolete. The result is *A Passion for Books*.

As many readers will be aware, I have borrowed my title from Lawrence Clark Powell's exquisite volume published in 1958. Like him, and like most of the contributors that follow, my own passion for books has been lifelong and real. I, too, grew up inside a home filled with books; my parents and grandparents and aunt were always reading, it seemed, and by their example they encouraged my brother and me to do the same. And so, in the solitude of our bedrooms, we had the privilege of reading uninterrupted to our hearts' content.

When television threatened to intrude, I was already caught fully by the intoxicating power of the printed word. The shallowness of much on the screen could not compare to the exhilarating journeys of the mind on which various authors took me, voyages to India, to Africa, to much of Europe, to most of America's states, to the Mayan Ruins, the Egyptian Pyramids, the Alps. I was entranced as I descended 20,000 leagues under the sea, stared into the eyes of a *Tyrannosaurus rex* and a raptor, climbed to the peak of Mount Everest, rode into orbit aboard a spaceship, and left my footprints in the dust of Mars, Venus, and Mercury. In other words, many delectable books took me out of my own life and into someone else's, and the sheer pleasure of that transposition remained with me as I became an adult and found new and even deeper ways to read, understand, and appreciate books. Little wonder that reading and writing have seemed for many of us not a chore or even a luxury, but instead an inevitability.

Perhaps concerns about what will become of the book in an electronic age are also inevitable. In *The Gutenberg Elegies*, Sven Bickerts suggests that 'everything in contemporary society discourages interiority.' Some commentators say that the endlessly diverting electronic advances of our visual and aural culture – radio, television, cinema, videos, CDs, CD-ROMs, miniaturization of whole libraries onto microchips, and the immense reach and scope of the World Wide Web – threaten to diminish the practice and pleasure of reading books. The fear is that reading in the classic sense may become, as George Steiner put it at the Publishers' Association Centenary Conference (29 March 1996), 'as specialized a skill and avocation as it was in the *scriptoria* and libraries of the monasteries during the so-called Dark Ages. The wish to attend to a demanding text, to master the grammar, the arts of memory, the tactics of repose and concentration, may once more become the practice of an elite, of a mandarinate of silences.' J. Hillis Miller adds: 'Media culture, disseminated globally, has the power to drown out the quiet voice of the fading book culture and also to blur the specificities of local and national societies.'

For my part I cannot agree that the day of the printed word is passing, and neither can many of the contributors to this volume. At a time when serious publishers are facing an acute crisis of identity, when some observers suspiciously regard reading books as an elitist and antiquated passion, more and more people are crowding into the stores, more new titles are published each year, and intense scholarly interest in the history of reading is increasing, not lessening. Films or television or computers will never do for us what books can do: they are convenient, durable, portable, self-sufficient; they can be read or carried anywhere; they can be ingested slowly in quiet solitude; they are available to everyone. 'Of all the inanimate objects, of all men's creations,' wrote Joseph Conrad in his autobiography, 'books are the nearest to us, for they contain our very thought, our ambitions, our indignations, our illusions, our fidelity to truth, and our persistent leaning toward error.' We can reread them, at our own pace, and reconsider what we've read. 'The convenience of the book . . . will ensure a long life for it,' says Robertson Davies, 'unless we bring up a race that has forgotten to read.' That concern, perhaps, is the subject of another anthology; what the writers in this one affirm is that the partnership between reader and book is a unique and invaluable one and that no glowing computer screen can replace the fundamental joy of holding a book in one's hands, pushing back its cover, and escaping into its pages.

How do books shape and nourish our inner lives? What motivates readers to turn to books in the era of cyberspace? What role do collectors play in the preservation of books? What are the central issues for academic publishers who are trying to preserve the book? Does the book have a future? These are among the questions answered in the essays that follow: some personal and anecdotal, some philosophical, others practical. Taken together, I hope that *A Passion for Books* will appeal to anyone who cares at all about the past and future of books and the publishing industry.

Quite obviously this book is a joint endeavor, and it goes without saying that I owe a special debt of gratitude to the contributors who, I am sure, would agree with Eric Burns when he says in *The Joy of Books*: 'Men and women who trust to books in the age of technology hold no special charms. They are as likely as anyone else to feel adrift from time to time, as likely to know the void of unanswered questions, the pain of unfulfilled ambitions, the waste of unspoken sentiments. But others may have nowhere to turn. The serious reader always has a place of his own.'

With book in hand, a reader is never alone. 'Old books, like old friends,' writes Michael Korda, 'are always the best of companions.'

Dale Salwak
Citrus College
Glendora, California

Acknowledgements

Grateful acknowledgement is made to the following for permission to reprint previously published materials:

Elizabeth Eisenstein and the editor for 'The End of the Book? Some Perspectives on Media Change,' *The American Scholar*, LXIV (1995) 541–55;

Joseph Epstein and the editor for 'The Pleasures of Reading,' *The Hudson Review*, XLVIII (1996) 539–55;

Mary Gordon and Random House for 'Reading My Father,' excerpted from *The Shadow Man* (1996).

Alan Sillitoe and W. H. Allen for 'Mountains and Caverns,' excerpted from *Mountains and Caverns* (1975).

Every effort has been made to trace all copyright-holders, but if any have been inadvertently overlooked the publishers will be pleased to make the necessary arrangement at the first opportunity.

Notes on the Contributors

Frances H. Bachelder, pianist and teacher for over forty years, studied at the University of Massachusetts and Purdue University. She now resides in San Diego, California, and while continuing her career as pianist also writes poetry and non-fiction. She is the author of essays on Barbara Pym, Anne Tyler, and the power of prayer, and of a book, *Mary Roberts Rinehart: Mistress of Mystery* (1993).

John Bayley is former Fellow and Tutor at New College, Oxford (1955–75) and Warton Professor of English Literature (1975–92). His publications include *The Romantic Survival: A Study in Poetic Evolution* (1956), *The Characters of Love* (1960), *Tolstoy and the Novel* (1965), *Pushkin: A Comparative Commentary* (1969), *The Uses of Division: Unity and Disharmony in Literature* (1973), *An Essay on Hardy* (1977), *The Line of Battle at Trafalgar* (essays, 1978), *Selected Essays* (1980), *Shakespeare and Tragedy* (1982) and *The Poetry of A. E. Housman* (1990). He has also published five novels: *Another Country* (1955), *Alice* (1994), *The Queer Captain* (1995), *George's Lair* (1996), and *The Red Hat* (1997). His latest book, *Elegy for Iris*, is a memoir of his wife, the novelist Iris Murdoch, and their joint fight against her Alzheimer's disease.

Gill Davies has worked in academic publishing for twenty-five years. She has been at Free Association Books – a small, independent publisher – for just over four years, working as Managing Director and Publisher. Before that she was Managing Director of Tavistock Publications, Publishing Director of Routledge, and Managing Director of Library Association Publishing. She was the first woman to be elected Chair of the Council for Academic Publishing and is an Honorary Lecturer of Cardiff University. She is the author of *Book Commissioning and Acquisition*, which was published in 1994, and which has since been translated into German, Chinese and Polish.

Margaret Drabble was born in Sheffield in 1939 and educated in York and Cambridge. Her first novel, *A Summer Birdcage*, was published in 1963. Since then she has published twelve novels including the trilogy *The Radiant Way* (1987), *A Natural Curiosity* (1989), and *The Gates of Ivory* (1991), which offers a panoramic view of Britain (and beyond) in Thatcher's 1980s. Her thirteenth novel, *The Witch of Exmoor*, appeared in 1996. Among her non-fiction works are biographies of Arnold Bennett (1974) and Angus Wilson (1995) and she edited the fifth edition of *The Oxford Companion to English Literature* (1985). Margaret Drabble has three children and three grandchildren, and is married to the biographer Michael Holroyd. She lives in London and Somerset.

Elizabeth L. Eisenstein was born and educated in New York City. She received her BA from Vassar College, her MA and PhD from Radcliffe. She served as Alice Freeman Palmer Professor of History at the University of Michigan 1975–88. Her two-volume work: *The Printing Press as an Agent of Change* (Cambridge, 1979), received the Ralph Waldo Emerson Phi Beta Kappa Prize. An abridged version: *The Printing Revolution in Early Modern Europe* (Cambridge, 1983), was reissued in 1993 as a 'Canto' paperback. Italian, French, Spanish, German and Japanese translations have appeared. Greek, Portuguese and Polish versions are forthcoming. The Lyell Lectures she gave at Oxford were published under the title: *Grub Street Abroad* (1992).

Michael Ellis graduated from Dartmouth College and earned a Certificat from the Sorbonne along the way. He spent the next thirty-five years working in the theatre as actor, stage manager and producer. He produced more than 250 plays, among them Neil Simon's first play, *Come Blow Your Horn*, and S. J. Perelman's last, *The Beauty Part*. At the age of sixty, Ellis began to study magic and for the past twenty years has been what is euphemistically called a 'semi-professional' magician. He was President of the International Brotherhood of Magicians, the largest magic organization in the world, in 1990–91.

Joseph Epstein has written twelve books and is the editor of *The Norton Book of Personal Essays*. He teaches in the Department of English at Northwestern University. For many years he edited *The American Scholar*.

Mary Gordon's novels have been bestsellers – *Final Payments*, *The Company of Women*, *Men and Angels*, *The Other Side*, and a memoir, *The Shadow Man*. She has published a book of novellas, *The Rest of Life*, a collection of stories, *Temporary Shelter*, and a book of essays, *Good Boys and Dead Girls*. She has received the Lila Acheson Wallace-Reader's Digest Writer's Award and a Guggenheim Fellowship. She is a professor of English at Barnard College.

Nina King has been the editor of *Book World*, the Sunday literary supplement of the *Washington Post* since 1988. She previously was book editor for *Newsday* in New York. Before becoming a journalist, King taught at universities in Detroit and New York. She is a graduate of the University of North Carolina and has a PhD in Victorian literature from Wayne State University. She has written numerous reviews and feature articles. Mystery fiction and Cuban culture are among her current special interests. A past president of the National Book Critics Circle, King is the principal author of *Crimes of the Scene: A Mystery Novel Guide for the International Traveler*.

Laurence Lerner, Fellow of the Royal Society of Literature, has taught at many universities. For more than twenty years he was on the faculty at the University of Sussex; in 1985 he went to Vanderbilt University as Kenan Professor of English, and retired in 1995. He is the author of three novels, nine volumes of poetry (of which the most recent is *Rembrandt's Mirror*, 1987), and many critical works, including *Love & Marriage: Literature in Its Social Context* (1979), *The Frontiers of Literature* (1988) and, most recently, *Angels and Absences: Child Deaths in the 19th Century* (1997). He now lives in Sussex.

Jeffrey Meyers, a Fellow of the Royal Society of Literature, has written biographies of Katherine Mansfield, Wyndham Lewis, Ernest Hemingway, Robert Lowell and his circle, D.H. Lawrence, Joseph Conrad, Edgar Allan Poe, Scott Fitzgerald, Edmund Wilson, Robert Frost, Humphrey Bogart and Gary Cooper. He lives in Berkeley, California.

Ferdinand Mount has been editor of *The Times Literary Supplement* since 1991. He was born in 1939 and educated at Eton and Christ Church, Oxford. He has worked for various newspapers and periodicals on both sides of the Atlantic, including *The Times*,

The Daily Telegraph, Encounter, The Spectator, and *National Review.* Between 1982 and 1984 he was head of the Prime Minister's Policy Unit. He is the author of *The Subversive Family* (1982), *The British Constitution Now* (1992), and of seven novels, among which *Of Love and Asthma* won the Hawthornden Prize for 1992.

Laura L. Nagy is a college administrator, instructor, and free-lance editor and writer living among the granite-faced hills and pristine forests of New Hampshire. A lifelong word-monger, she has worked in newspaper, magazine, and book publishing, and has taught writing, literature, communications, and journalism at several American colleges and universities. She still prizes her childhood copy of Dr. Seuss's *On Beyond Zebra* because she thinks it addresses significant philosophical issues, chief among them how to break free from self-imposed limitations.

Catherine Peters is the author of *The King of Inventors: A Life of Wilkie Collins* (Secker & Warburg, 1991; Princeton, 1993), *Thackeray's Universe* (Faber and Faber; Oxford University Press 1987), and *Charles Dickens: A Pocket Biography* (Alan Sutton, 1998). During the 1960s and '70s she worked in publishing in London, and from 1981 to 1992 taught nineteenth- and twentieth-century English literature at Somerville College, Oxford. She now spends her time reading, writing, gardening, and playing with and reading to her grandchildren. She is a Fellow of the Royal Society of Literature.

Dale Salwak is Professor of English at Southern California's Citrus College. He was educated at Purdue University (BA) and then the University of Southern California (MA, PhD) under a National Defense Education Act competitive fellowship program. In 1985 he was awarded a National Endowment for the Humanities grant. In 1987 Purdue University awarded him its Distinguished Alumni Award. His publications include *The Literary Biography: Problems and Solutions* (1996) and studies of Kingsley Amis, John Braine, A.J. Cronin, Philip Larkin, Barbara Pym, Carl Sandburg, Anne Tyler, and John Wain. He is now completing a literary study of the English Bible.

James Shapiro is Professor of English and Comparative Litera-ture at Columbia University. He is the author of *Rival Playwrights* and *Shakespeare and the Jews* and co-editor of *The Columbia Anthology of British Poetry*.

Alan Sillitoe's novels include *Saturday Night and Sunday Morning* (1958), *The Loneliness of the Long Distance Runner* (1959), *The General* (1960), *The Death of William Posters* (1965), and *A Tree on Fire* (1967). His most recent books are an autobiography, *Life Without Armour* (1996), a collection of short stories, *Alligator Playground* (1997) and a new novel, *The Broken Chariot* (1998).

G. Thomas Tanselle, Vice President of the John Simon Guggenheim Memorial Foundation and Adjunct Professor of English and Comparative Literature at Columbia University, has written and lectured extensively on analytical bibliography, printing and publishing history, textual criticism, book collecting, and other aspects of books as physical objects. He also writes on American literature (his first book was on Royall Tyler) and is one of three co-editors of the Northwestern-Newberry Edition of *The Writings of Herman Melville* (1968–). His most recent books include *A Rationale of Textual Criticism* (1989), *Textual Criticism and Scholarly Editing* (1990), and *Literature and Artifacts* (1998).

Ann Thwaite was born in London but her parents came from New Zealand and she spent the war years there, returning to finish her education in England, taking her degree at Oxford in 1955. She published many children's books before writing her first biography: *Waiting for the Party: the Life of Frances Hodgson Burnett* (1974). *Edmund Gosse: A Literary Landscape* won the Duff Cooper Prize for 1985, and *A. A. Milne: His Life* was the Whitbread Biography of the Year, 1990. She is a Fellow of the Royal Society of Literature, and a Churchill Fellowship allowed her to travel widely when researching her latest biography: *Emily Tennyson, the Poet's Wife* (1996). In 1998 she was awarded a D.Litt by Oxford University and the Gladys Krieble Delmas Fellowship at the British Library. She is married to the poet Anthony Thwaite.

Part One
Contemporary Trends

1

The Pleasures of Reading

JOSEPH EPSTEIN

Five or six years ago, I was informed by my literary agent that two of my books were to be recorded by a firm called Books on Tape. Although the advance was not such as to earn me an honorable discharge from the financial wars, this was nonetheless pleasing news. Five or six months later, two smallish boxes arrived with the actual tapes. Ah, thought I, now here is a scrumptious little snack for the ego. I shall play these tapes in my car as I drive around Chicago, or on the Indiana Tollway, or up the Pacific Coast Highway. How soothing, how delicious the prospect, driving along and listening to that most amusing of people, oneself, or at least one's own thoughts. Wasn't it Philip Larkin who said that sex was altogether too good to share with anyone else? Listening to oneself on tape seemed the literary equivalent of Larkin's sentiment. Onan, I'm phonin', dear boy, to say you don't know the half of it. Or so I had supposed.

When I slipped my first tape into the tape player in my car, waiting for the lush cascade of words – my words, every last darling one among them – I was aquiver with anticipation. Cutting now directly to the chase, allow me to tell you that I didn't end up wrapped round a telephone pole, a silly grin of ecstasy on my face. No, I never made it through the first tape – I never made it, in fact, through even the first five minutes of the first tape. As it turned out, the man assigned to record my books had an odd, slightly twerpy accent; his rhythms were not mine; and listening to him rattle on, rolling obliviously over my careful punctuation – all this was more than I felt I could take.

I have since had four other of my books recorded on Books on Tape. The most recent of these has been a book of short stories, which contains ten or twelve Yiddish words that the (I assume under-employed) actor hired by Books on Tape, in his conscientiousness,

3

actually called to get official pronunciations of – such words as *mishagoss, nurishkeit, mishpacha*. But I found I could not listen to these tapes, either. I didn't even open the boxes in which they arrived. What is going on here? I know lots of intelligent people who listen to books on tape with intellectual profit and simple amusement. Why can't I?

Before getting round to an answer, let me go on to a further confession: I cannot read detective or spy fiction. It is not that, along with Edmund Wilson, I don't care who killed Roger Ackroyd – though I guess, deep down, I really don't care all that much – but that I just don't care to read about it. It is not my immitigable highbrowism, for my highbrowism turns out to be pretty easily mitigated. I don't in the least mind watching detective or spy stories in the movies or on television. Some of the best Holly-wood movies – *Double Indemnity, The Maltese Falcon, Farewell, My Lovely, The Day of the Jackal* – have been detective and spy stories, with the rest probably westerns; and while I wouldn't think to read a Tom Clancy novel, at my regular evening post as couch potato I find I am able to watch VCR versions of his movies and feel, as is nowadays said, hey, no pain whatsoever. I just can't bear to read the stuff.

The problem for me is that reading is I won't say a sacred but nevertheless a pretty serious act. A very sensual act it is, too. I take account of the look, feel, even smell of a book. I like, or feel uncomfortable with, its heft in my hand. In reading, pace means a great deal, and one of the good things about a book, as opposed to a tape, is that you can read it at your own pace: flying on by, stopping, re-reading, even nodding, nodding more frequently, till – *ka-boom* – the book drops from your hand.

I read, for the most part, very slowly. The very notion of speed-reading is repugnant to me. ('Read *Anna Karenina* last night,' an old joke about speed-reading has it. 'A book set in Russia, isn't it?') The better the book, the more slowly I tend to read it. The older I get, also the more slowly I read – not so much because my mental faculties begin to break down, which I'm sure they do, but because I am no longer so confident, as when younger I was, that I have a respectable chance of returning to re-read the book in my hand. Besides, the notion of speed-reading is doubly repugnant for speeding up a pleasure. If speed-reading were really to catch on, can speed-eating be far behind? Let us not speak of other pleasurable activities.

In a brief piece in *The New Yorker*, Benjamin Cheever, a great devotee of listening to books on tape, recounts that he not only listens to books on a tape player in his car but walks around the house wearing a Walkman 'so that I can listen to a book while I run, rinse the dishes, make coffee, or shave.' I myself rarely leave the house without a book, and I have been known to read a few paragraphs in the elevator in our building, or possibly finish a page or two while in line at the bank, and even catch a quick paragraph in my car at a longish stoplight. But whenever, or wherever I read, I need a pencil nearby to make my inevitable sideline of something I consider important, or plan to return to, or need to look up. I sometimes copy out things from books I am reading in a commonplace book I keep. I cannot depart from a book until I have a distinct sense of my place, and usually prefer not to cease reading until I arrive at the beginning of the first full paragraph on the left-hand page. You may think me very anal, but I need to observe all these little idiosyncracies. ('Anality!' a character in an English novel exclaims when accused of it. 'Anality – my ass!')

Being a writer also makes me a slower reader. Anyone – and I exclude only Ludwig Wittgenstein from this proposition – who reads a sentence has to make the following little check on it: 1. Is it clear? 2. Is it (grammatically, semantically, logically) correct? 3. Is it interesting? 4. Is it true? 5. Is it (charming bonus) beautiful? And then, if he or she is a writer, three further questions arise: 1. How was it made? 2. Could it be improved? and 3. What, for my own writing, can I steal from it? I have never met a good writer who wasn't also a penetrating reader; and every good writer, with varying degrees of consciousness and subtlety, is also a plagiarist.

Shocking to report, now past sixty, I still do not know all the words in the English language. The other morning I was reading Owen Chadwick's fine book *Britain and the Vatican during the Second World War* and came upon Chadwick's description of Myron Taylor, President Roosevelt's personal envoy to Pope Pius XII, as 'rhadamanthine.' It bugs me not to know a word. I am content not to know the meaning of the universe, or why God sent sin or suffering into the world, but not to know what a word means is beyond my tolerance. I trust you will think me on this matter altogether too rhadamanthine, which is to say, severe, or strict, coming from the judge Rhadamanthus in Hades in Greek mythology. But there it is, a tic, and I am stuck with it.

I am also stuck, though at last becoming slowly unstuck, with the notion of finishing any book I begin and of reading every blasted word of it. I was pleased, some years ago, to discover that Justice Holmes, a wonderfully penetrating reader of excellent taste, suffered the same affliction until the age of seventy-five. Behind this was Holmes's worry that, at the gates of heaven, St. Peter would quiz him about his reading, and he didn't want to be caught saying he had read a book that he hadn't really finished. I read this in one of the collections of Justice Holmes's letters, of all of which, take my word on it, I have read every word.

I have at long last arrived at the age of skimming, which I still don't do with an altogether clear conscience. But why, I now tell myself, should I suffer painful *longueurs* in novels, too-lengthy plot summaries in biographies of novelists, long quotations from third-rate sources. I may be beautiful, as the blues song has it, but I'm goin' to die someday, and, I now say to myself, how 'bout some better readin', before I pass away.

The notion that, *mirabile dictu*, I am going to die someday, now all too realistic, makes me more cautious in what I choose to read. I am handed an eight-hundred-page biography and am now forced to consider that reading such a book entails at least two weeks out of my reading life. Do I wish to make the investment? Suddenly this has become a fairly serious question.

Gertrude Stein said that the happiest moment of her life was that moment in which she realized she wouldn't be able to read all the books in the world. I suppose what made it happy for her was that it took off a fair amount of pressure. I have finally come to the realization that I shan't be able to read even all the good books in the world, and, far from making me happy, it leaves me, a naturally acquisitive fellow, a little sad. It does make rather more pressing, once one grants a world of limited possibilities, the question of which books one ought to read and which exclude.

The late Alexander Gershenkron, an economic historian at Harvard, once took up the matter of how much one can read in a lifetime, and with rather depressing statistical consequences. Gershenkron was then near seventy, and he estimated that, in his adult life, which he felt began at the age of twenty, he read roughly two books (outside of his professional reading) a week. This meant that, over fifty years of reading, one will have read only five thousand or so books. A piddling sum, when one real-

izes that something like fifty-five thousand books are published
annually in the United States alone.

Given this daunting logistical problem, Gershenkron, in an essay
in *The American Scholar*, remarked that it is a shame to have read
too many of the wrong books, and so set out to discover criteria
for establishing which are the right – or best – books. He arrived
at three criteria, and these are: 1. a book should be intrinsically
interesting; 2. a book should be re-readable; and 3. a book should
be memorable. These criteria are thoughtful, impeccable, and, as
by now you may have noticed, utterly useless. How, after all,
can one know if a book is interesting until one has read well
into it, or re-readable until one has read it through a second time,
or memorable until long after one has finished reading it? One can't.

Advice about books has always been plentiful. The more practical the better I like it. The *Wall Street Journal* columnist Irving
Kristol used to tell students at the NYU Business School never to
show up for a job interview carrying a novel, which seems to
me very sound advice, unless you happen to be interviewing for
the job of literary critic or novelist. The late Arnaldo Momigliano,
the great historian of the ancient world, once told me, in his
strong Piedmontese accent, 'You know, the cheapest way to acquire
a book remains to buy it.' I puzzled over that for an hour or
two, before figuring out that what Arnaldo meant was that if
you bought a book, rather than have it given or lent to you, at
least you weren't under any obligation to read the damn thing.

Perhaps in America, where cultural confidence has always been
a bit shaky, advice about what one ought to read has also been
especially plentiful. As early as 1771, a man named Robert Skipwith,
who was to be Mrs. Jefferson's brother-in-law, asked the then
twenty-eight-year-old Thomas Jefferson to draw up a list of books
'suited to the capacity of a common reader who understands but
little of the classicks and who has not leisure for any intricate or
tedious study. Let them [these books] be improving and amusing.'
Jefferson obliged with a list of 148 books, mostly in the classics
but with a few intensely practical works, among them a book on
horse-hoeing husbandry and Nourse's *Compendium of Physic and
Surgery*.

The flow of such advice since has never ceased. There was
Harvard's once famous five-foot shelf of classics and, later,
Encyclopaedia Britannica's *Great Books of the Western World*. In
the early 1980s, a book was published titled *The List of Books: A*

Library of Over 3,000 Works. By the time it was published, of course, the list was dated, being filled with books of that day on politics and popular culture: instructing one on the importance of the novels of Kurt Vonnegut, the Vietnam history of Frances Fitzgerald, Frantz Fanon's *The Wretched of the Earth,* and other books that one now turns away from at the asking price of 25 cents at garage sales.

No one, I fear, can offer much useful advice on what you ought to read, apart from making the important distinction between serious and unserious books. I once suggested in an essay that certain books were age specific – that is, that certain books ought or ought not to be read before or beyond certain ages: no Thomas Wolfe after eighteen; no F. Scott Fitzgerald beyond thirty, no Chekhov before thirty; no Proust before forty; no James Joyce beyond fifty – that sort of thing. Perhaps the best and only worthwhile distinction is that made by a character in an R. K. Narayan novel, who divided his personal library into good books and bad. In mystical fact, books have a mysterious, unpatterned way of appearing when one needs them. Or so at least they have in my life.

I grew up in an almost entirely unbookish home. Although neither of my parents was an immigrant, and both were well-spoken, I don't remember there being an English dictionary in our apartment. Magazines and newspapers were around in plenty. Only two books were kept, these in many copies, and both were stored in the basement. These were books written by my grandfather, in Yiddish and Hebrew, published in Montreal, where he lived, and subsidized in good part by my father. Whenever someone visited us who read Hebrew or Yiddish, I was instructed to run down to the basement to supply him or her with one of my grandfather's seemingly never diminishing stock of books.

I mention all this even though it does a bit of damage to one of the more pleasing stereotypes about Jews – that they are all bookish, artistic, sensitive, intellectual, born with something I can only call a culture gene. I grew up in a mostly Jewish neighborhood in which this gene seems never to have shown up. None of my boyhood friends was a reader, and neither was I. None of us played the piano, and certainly not the violin, that Jewish instrument *par excellence.* What we played were American sports, and what we yearned to be was wise in the ways of the modern city. The sons of moderately successful businessmen, we were adolescent gamblers and artful dodgers who hoped to grow into savvy men over whose eyes no one could pull the wool (make that cashmere).

Lonely children, or at least lonely boys, read books, and I was never lonely. A story is told about Edmund Wilson, whose mother worried that her son spent altogether too much time with books, and so bought him a baseball uniform and glove – in which the young Wilson suited up and promptly sat under a tree in the family's yard in Red Bank, New Jersey, where he continued reading. If my mother, going in the opposite route from Mrs. Wilson, had given me a set of books, I should probably have used them as bases and to mark the foul lines.

When a boy I read a book or two – *Hans Brinker and the Silver Skates*, *Black Beauty* – but for the most part my reading consisted of comic books and a publication still in circulation called *Sport Magazine*. When it came time to give book reports, I cheated by giving them from Classic Comics. When we were in, I believe, the fifth grade, a woman from the Chicago Public Library visited our school and, in a treacly accent, told us, 'Boys and girls, *boooks* are your friends. They will take you to unknown shores and reveal to you hitherto hidden treasures. Yes, boys and girls, *boooks* truly are your friends, so you must never bend their backs or write in their margins or dog-ear their pages.' This most impressive little talk put me off serious reading for at least another full five years.

I have since come not only to agree with the library lady, to whom I owe an apology, but to go a step further with Marcel Proust, who in his essay 'On Reading' claims, with some justification, that books, at least as company, are really superior to friends. One need engage in no small talk with a book, as Proust noted, no greetings in the hall, no expressions of gratitude, or excuses for delayed meetings. With books, unlike with friends, no sense of obligation exists. We are with them only because we absolutely wish to be with them. Nor do we have to laugh, politely, at their attempts at wit. As Proust says, 'No more deference: we laugh at what Molière says only to the degree that we find him funny; when he bores us, we are not afraid to appear bored, and when we decidedly have had enough of being with him, we put him back in his place as bluntly as if he had neither genius nor fame.'

We may even, in extreme conditions, and contra the library lady, break the back and dog-ear the hell out of a book, which we certainly cannot do to friends. Besides, as you cannot with a friend, you can deal with a book at the pace you prefer: maundering, skimming, or plowing straight through. You can argue with a book, or even curse it, and not have to worry about being put down by a superior mind. (An Evanston bookseller once told me that he was much amused with a book that came into his shop that contained, in the margin of one of its pages, the remark, 'C'mon, Ortega!')

The first book that really, that deeply, engaged my interest arrived when I was thirteen. It had a thick red cover, trimmed in black, and was titled *All-American*. It was written by a man named John R. Tunis, and was, as I had hoped it would be, about football – high-school football. It was illustrated by a man named Hans Walleen, had a protagonist named Meyer Goldman, a Jewish halfback (anti-Semitism was part of the story), and was so immensely readable that I lapped up its 250 fairly large-print pages in a single day. As we should say nowadays, it blew me away.

How to recover what Marcel Proust calls the original psychological act of reading? I am not sure I can do it justice. I remember being swept up in John R. Tunis' story. I remember pulling for characters – wanting them to win through. I remember wanting to rush to the end of the story, to make sure it ended in a victory for goodness, fairness, and decency (not to worry, it did). At the same time that I wanted to know how things worked out, I didn't really want the book to end and so to be ejected from this swell world that John R. Tunis created.

All-American did something that not many other things I had thus far encountered in life were able to do – it took me out of myself and put me into a larger world. Not all that much larger, now that I come to think about it, but larger enough to stir my imagination. Even the details of reading the book return to me, forty-five years later. I read part of it in our living room, and finished it, supine, propped up on my bed, on top of the spread, leaning on my right elbow.

I can remember the conditions surrounding the reading of lots of books that had a strong effect on me as a boy. I remember sitting up all night, in the bed next to which my father slept in the Brown Hotel in Des Moines, Iowa, where at sixteen I had gone with him on business, to finish Willard Motley's *Knock on Any Door*; I remember sitting, legs crossed Indian style, reading John Dos Passos' *U.S.A.* in a park called Indian Boundary on the northside of Chicago. I remember reading *Catcher in the Rye* on a train headed for Champaign, Illinois. Oddly, I don't remember the conditions under which I read *The Grapes of Wrath*, another key book for me in my youth.

All of these books I read with no sense of their quality or place in the general hierarchy of critical importance, for these things, pleasant to report, had not yet any meaning for me; these books excited me because they seemed to take hold of life, and consequently they took hold of me.

Proust, that brilliant anatomist of passion, recalled everything about his own reading experience, about which he reports both in *Remembrance of Things Past* and in 'On Reading.' Characteristically, he laments the passing of the intense pleasure that his boyish reading gave him. Reporting on his emotions upon the completion of a book, he writes:

> Then, what? This book, it was nothing but that? Those beings [its characters] to whom one had given more of one's attention and tenderness than to people in real life, not always daring to admit how much one loved them, even when our parents found us reading and appeared to smile at our emotions, so that we closed the book with affected indifference or feigned ennui; those people, for whom one had panted and sobbed, one would never see again, one would no longer know anything about them.

'How do you manage to know so many things, Monsieur France?' Proust is supposed to have asked Anatole France, to which the older writer is said to have replied: 'It's quite simple, my dear Marcel. When I was your age, I wasn't good-looking and popular like you. So instead of going into society I stayed at home and did nothing but read.' Later in life, given a choice, would Marcel have preferred going to a party or staying home with a book? It would depend, I suppose he might have answered, on who was giving the party and whether certain duchesses would be there. And of course much later in life, he preferred to stay home to write a book that has kept many of us at home reading it for weeks on end.

I ought to have known that I was in danger of being seriously hooked on books and the pleasures of reading when, one sunny summer afternoon in my fourteenth year, I stayed home to read another John R. Tunis novel, this one about baseball. When I could as easily have been outside playing the game, I preferred at that moment to continue reading about it. A bookworm, clearly, was in the making.

Still, the hook took a while to sink in. I read scarcely at all in high school, and then mainly books about the slums. *The Amboy Dukes* by Irving Schulman, a novel about a bunch of thuggish kids in Brooklyn, was a much thumbed book in my high school. In print – in actual print in those happily prudish times – it used the word 'jugs' to refer to a girl's breasts. I read other books in this general line of hoods in the slum books, including one actually called *The Hoods*, by a man named Harry Grey, from which, owing to the perverse games that memory chooses to play, I still recall the sentence, 'Cockneyed Hymie at the wheel, the big boat pulled into the night and I thrilled to the sensation of the clutch.'

Although I was never a good student, the University of Chicago did teach me which were the important books. I was, though, pleased to depart that exalted setting so that I might read, alongside all those great books, a number of merely good ones, of my own choosing and to be read in my own unsystematic way. My own unsystematic way included a few key motives, among them reading to discover what life was supposed to be like and how one was supposed to live it. 'Genius,' wrote Henry James, 'is only the art of getting your experience fast, of stealing it, as it were.' I hoped to steal a lot of experience from books, and believe I may have done so. Then, too, the question implicit in reading every great writer, or so I began to sense, is, What would he or she have thought of me? Reading a serious book, it turns out, provides a way of reconsidering one's own life from the author's perspective.

I have never clocked myself here, but my guess is that rare is the day that I do not spend anywhere from three to five hours reading. Apart from ablutions and making coffee, reading is the first thing I do in the morning and generally the last thing I do at night. I once tried to go a day without reading and found it compared in difficulty of deprivation with going a day without smoking; and I speak as a former two-pack-a-day man. My children seem to recall the most repeated phrase from their growing up with me as their father being, 'One moment: I'll be with you as soon as I finish this paragraph.' Whenever I am abroad, in no matter how exotic the city – Athens, Constantinople, Jerusalem – at some point I yearn to stay the day in the hotel room and do nothing but read.

I am always amused to note, when the *New York Times* prints one of its Man or Woman in the News pieces, one of these men or women listing under hobbies such items as 'Tennis, Travel, *Reading*.' The notion of reading as a hobby to one for whom it is very nearly a way of life is comically absurd. With any luck at all, I shall never be the Man in the News, but if I am, I should as readily list under my hobbies, 'Tennis, Travel, and *Breathing*.' Hilton Kramer, another voracious reader, has more than once remarked of certain jobs – in government, as directors of large museums and other cultural institutions, as presidents of universities – that they are among those jobs 'which never allow you to read another book.' A poet, a Russian proverb has it, always cheats his boss. A really serious reader, a proverb I have invented for this occasion, is probably better off not being a boss.

I don't wish to make my own reading seem grim, a lonely quest for wisdom, a form of psychotherapy by other (and less expensive) means, onward ever onward, beating on, boats against the current, working in the dark, my passion my task . . . and the rest of it. On the contrary. My motives in reading are thoroughly mixed, but pure pleasure is always high among them. I read for aesthetic pleasure. If anything, with the passing of years, I have become sufficiently the aesthetic snob so that I can scarcely drag my eyes across the pages of a badly or even pedestrianly written book. I count myself one of Henry James's little band, 'partakers of the same repose, who sit together in the shade of the tree, by the splash of the fountain, with the glare of the desert around us and no great vice that I know of but the habit perhaps of estimating people a little too much by what they think of a certain style.' Along with the love of style, I read in the hope of laughter, exaltation, insight, enhanced consciousness, and dare I say it, *wisdom*; I read, finally, hoping to get a little smarter about the world.

Such are my hopes. But what, exactly, do I actually get out of this activity on which I spend three to five hours daily? What is the point? I explain to my students that I by now have probably forgotten more than they have read – a remark made not in a spirit of braggadocio but in literal truth and true regret. There are whole – and entirely serious – novels I have read about which I cannot recall a thing. One such is Dostoevsky's *The Idiot*. All I can tell you about that thick book is that its protagonist is a man named Prince Myshkin, he is an epileptic, and, in ways I cannot recall, somehow wise in his innocence. Otherwise: total blank, nada, zilch. Read *The Idiot* roughly thirty years ago – a novel set in Russia, isn't it?

Plots do not stay all that long in my mind. I do not, as a previous generation did, memorize vast stretches of poetry. What I consciously take away from many of the books I read are scenes, oddments, bits and pieces. I am somehow less interested in the final meaning of T. S. Eliot's 'The Love Song of J. Alfred Prufrock' than I am in the fact that so many of the phrases from that poem have stuck in my mind for more than forty years. From an Isaac Bashevis Singer story, I recall the earlock of a yeshiva student, flapping in the wind; I remember the little finger of Father Sergius, in Tolstoy's story of that name, twirling in the air after he has chopped it off in his struggle to hold sensuality at bay; I remember the hero of one of Henry Miller's novels – one of the *Tropics* – making love standing up in a hallway in Paris when a coin drops from his companion's purse and the Miller narrator remarks to himself, 'I made a mental note to pick it up later'; in Owen Chadwick's *Britain and the Vatican during the Second World War*, I already suspect that, in the years to come, I shall only recall the diary entry of the British envoy to the Vatican, D'Arcy Osborne, who, unable to leave the Vatican while Italy was at war with England, noted: 'I reached the grave conclusion during the mass that I am nothing but a pencilled marginal note in the Book of Life. I am not in the main text at all.'

Reading is always at its best for me when the writer makes of it a sheath of words with which to capture the rich, unpredictable, astonishing flow of life. The metaphor of the sheath comes from Willa Cather, who in *The Song of the Lark* has her opera-singer-heroine Thea Kronborg, while standing in a stream in the pueblo country, reflect: '. . . what was any art but an effort to make a sheath, a mould in which to imprison for a moment, the shining, elusive element which is life itself – life hurrying past us and running away, too strong to stop, too sweet to lose?'

Not only am I unclear about what the main text of the Book of Life is, but I am not always entirely sure what the main texts of actual books are. Am I, I wonder, insufficiently interested in such ideas as works of literature may be said to contain? There are those, and I am among them, who claim that, when it is going at its best, literature sails above the realm of ideas anyhow.

'He had a mind so fine no idea could violate it,' said T. S. Eliot of Henry James. By that lovely rhythmic formulation I take Eliot to mean not that James was incapable of grasping or of functioning at the level of ideas, but instead that his true interest was elsewhere. James, Eliot is saying, was not interested in the knowledge contained in the various ideas or 'isms' of literature, but in the truths known to the human heart and soul, the truths of sensibility – interested, that is, in what for the artist are the higher truths.

T. S. Eliot, at the age of thirty, writing to his friend Mary Hutchinson, allowed that there were two ways in which one ought to read: '1) because of particular and personal interest, which makes the thing one's own, regardless of what other people think of the book, 2) *to a certain extent*, because it is something that one "ought to have read" – but one must be quite clear that this is *why* one is reading.' Eliot goes on to say that, apropos of reading, there are two kinds of intelligence: 'the intellectual and the sensitive – the first can read a great deal because it schematises and theorizes – the second not much, because it requires one to get more out of a book than can immediately be put into words.' He then adds that '*I* read very little – and *have* read much less than people think – at present I only read Tudor drama, Tudor prose, and Gibbon – over and over – when I have time to read at all. Of course I don't count the countless books I have to skim for lectures, etc.'

Marguerite Yourcenar said that there were three sources of knowledge in the world: that knowledge which comes from observing fellow human beings, that knowledge which comes from looking into one's heart, and that knowledge which comes from books. Is there any point in ranking the three according to importance? I suspect not. Not to observe others is to put oneself in danger in the world, not to observe oneself is to lose the permanent use of that un-named organ responsible for reflection, not to read is to risk barbarizing oneself – leave any one of the three out and you have a less than fully equipped human being.

I am not sure Marcel Proust would agree. He had strong notions about the limitations of reading. He thought reading especially useful to the indolent mind, which cannot think in solitude, but requires the lubrication of another, superior mind to set its own in thoughtful motion. My guess is that Proust thought his own a mind of this kind. I know my own is; if my thoughts are ever to catch fire, I need to rub them up against those of a finer grained mind than my own.

Proust thought that the true point of reading was to waken us to the life of the spirit. The danger in reading, he felt, was when it tended to substitute itself for this life of the spirit – when, as he wrote, 'truth no longer appears to us as an ideal we can realize only through the intimate progress of our thought and the effort of our heart, but as a material thing, deposited between the leaves of books like honey ready-made by others, and which we have only to take the trouble of reaching for on the shelves of libraries and then savouring passively in perfect repose of body and mind.'

Yet this danger, of substituting books for intelligence, Proust thought, grew less as intelligence grew greater. Once we knew that we could 'develop the power of our sensibility and our intelligence only within ourselves, in the depths of our spiritual life,' books become, as Proust calls it, 'the noblest of distractions, the most ennobling one of all, for only reading and knowledge produce the "good manners" of the mind.'

I suppose one can accept Proust's strictures on the limitation of books, with this one qualification: how does the flame of intelligence grow greater without the substantial kindling of books to ignite it? Sometimes, too, more than mere intelligence is ignited by reading.

Consider, for example, the following scene: a very nervous young black man, not long up from Mississippi, appears at the desk of a branch library in the city of Memphis, Tennessee. He has forged a note, asking the librarian to give him some of the books of H. L. Mencken, an author whose name he had come across in that morning's paper. (It is the late 1920s, and the reason the note has to be forged is that blacks are not allowed to use the Memphis public library.) After a very nervous-making exchange, the young black man, whose name happens to be Richard Wright, is given two Mencken titles: one of these is *A Book of Prefaces*. Wright, in *Black Boy*, his autobiography, provides an account of the effect of his reading H. L. Mencken for the first time:

> That night in my rented room, while letting the hot water run over my can of pork and beans in the sink, I opened *A Book of Prefaces* and began to read. I was jarred and shocked by the style, the clear, clean sweeping sentences. Why did he write

like this? And how did one write like that? I pictured the man as a raging demon, slashing with his pen, consumed with hate, denouncing everything American, extolling everything European or German, laughing at the weakness of people, mocking God, authority. What was this? I stood up, trying to realize what reality lay behind the meaning of the words. . . . Yes, this man was fighting, fighting with words. He was using words as a weapon, using them as one would use a club. Could words be weapons? Well, yes, for here they were. Then, maybe, perhaps, I could use them as a weapon? No. It frightened me. I read on and what amazed me was not what he said, but how on earth anybody had the courage to say it.

Richard Wright continues:

I ran across many words whose meaning I did not know, and I either looked them up in a dictionary or, before I had a chance to do that, encountered the word in a context that made its meaning clear. But what strange world was this? I concluded the book with the conviction that I had somehow overlooked something terribly important in life. I had once tried to write, had once reveled in feeling, had let my crude imagination roam, but the impulse to dream had been slowly beaten out of me by experience. Now it surged up again and I hungered for books, new ways of looking and seeing. It was not a matter of believing or disbelieving what I read, but of feeling something new, of being affected by something that made the world look different.

Let me italicize Richard Wright's phrase *the impulse to dream*, which, he says, 'had been beaten out of me.' At times, much less brutally than in ways the young Richard Wright had to undergo I grant you, life beats it out of all of us. And books, 'that noblest distraction,' can replace it, sometimes in direct, sometimes in subtle ways.

Because I was born into a family with a strong practical cast, which I cannot shake off, nor want to, I have to ask myself what does all my reading mean? What does it come to? Again I ask: What is the point of spending so much time, on my duff, a book in my hand, reading vast quantities of lovely prose and poetry, much of which I shall probably forget?

I have asked this same question of my students. For the better part of four years, I say to them, you have read a mass of poems, plays, novels – what does it all come down to? Their answers, though not unintelligent, are a bit predictable. All this reading sharpens their minds, they say; it tends to put them in touch with noble ideals; it lets them experience things that, without books, they could never experience (the eighteenth century, for example). All these answers, though a mite platitudinous, are nevertheless correct. I have the advantage over them of at least making a living off all my reading. But does all their reading come together, does it add up to something at least philosophically if not commercially useful? Is there, in the impatient phrase of the day, a bottom line? Here, in searching for an answer, they stumble. I'm sure I couldn't have answered it myself at twenty or twenty-one, but I should like to attempt to do so now.

A fair amount of reading, of a belletristic kind, I have come to believe, confers on one – or at least ought to confer on one – what I think of as 'the literary point of view.' This point of view, which is taught not by any specific book or author, or even set of authors, teaches a worldly-wise skepticism, which comes through first in a distrust of general ideas. 'As soon as one creates a concept,' says Ortega, 'reality leaves the room.' (Right on, Ortega! I hope someone will write in the margin of this essay.) The literary point of view is distrustful of general ideas and above all of systems of ideas. It teaches, as Henry James advises, that you should 'never say that you know the last word about any human heart.' It teaches one to hold with Chekhov, who favored no sides or classes but wrote: 'I believe in individuals, I see salvation in isolated personalities scattered here and there throughout Russia; whether they're intellectuals or peasants, they are our strength, few of them though there are.'

The most complex lesson the literary point of view teaches – and it is not, to be sure, a lesson available to all, and is even difficult to keep in mind once acquired – is to allow the intellect to become subservient to the heart. What wide reading teaches is the richness, the complexity, the mystery of life. In the wider and longer view, I have come to believe, there is something deeply apolitical – something above politics – in literature, despite what feminist, Marxist, and other politicized literary critics may think. If at the end of a long life of reading the chief message you bring away is that women have had it lousy, or that capitalism stinks, or that attention must above all be paid to victims, then I'd say you just might have missed something crucial. Too bad, for there probably isn't time to go back to re-read your lifetime's allotment of 5,000 or so books.

People who have read with love and respect understand that the larger message behind all books, great and good and even some not so good as they might be, is, finally, cultivate your sensibility so that you may trust your heart. The charmingly ironic point of vast reading, at least as I have come to understand it, is to distrust much of one's education. Unfortunately, the only way to know this is first to become educated, just as the only way properly to despise success is first to achieve it.

Let me return and give all but the last word to Marcel Proust, who wrote:

> Our intellect is not the most subtle, the most powerful, the most appropriate instrument for revealing the truth. It is life that, little by little, example by example, permits us to see that what is most important to our heart, or to our mind, is learned not by reasoning, but through other agencies. Then it is that the intellect, observing their superiority, abdicates its control to them upon reasoned grounds and agrees to become their collaborator and lackey.

That seems to me impressively subtle, immensely smart, very wise. I came upon it, you may not be astonished to learn, in a book.

2

Other Worlds to Inhabit

JOHN BAYLEY

Gore Vidal has remarked that there are no true readers today, only would-be writers. Everyone wants to write a novel: nobody really wants to read one. Why should this be so? Of course like all such neat and sweeping generalizations it isn't really true, but it does none the less suggest a truth, and a trend. In spite of all rumours to the contrary fiction today is alive and well. Blockbusters appear as regularly as ever: the Great American novel continues to be hailed once a year or so, and before a successor replaces it sells a million copies. Exciting new novelists are always being discovered, together with dynamic and vital social and regional genres – the Canadian novel, the Australian novel, the Indian novel . . . All produce new and vigorous styles of vernacular English. What could be better suited to the expanding culture of our pluralistic society?

And yet something seems to be wrong, and not only in the view of a discerning old cynic like Vidal. Publishers are gloomy. After their dynamic expansion in the sixties and seventies, and their adoption of new and exciting styles and techniques of theory and criticism, English departments at the universities seem to have shrunk into humdrum normality, and a sort of fatalistic quiescence. Their students read less and less and rely more and more on a few set texts and standardized handbooks of criticism. It is perfectly possible now to do respectably well on an English course without reading any complete books at all, or developing a taste for reading and discovering them. Instead there has developed an almost unhealthy interest in Do It Yourself methods: how to write your own book has become of more pressing concern than learning to enjoy the work of others.

There's nothing to be done about it of course. Things are as they are and happen as they do happen, as Wittgenstein observed, and nowhere does this apply as much as in the cultural context. People – the young especially – will do what comes most naturally, which means what technology today offers. We cannot return to the past, or animate artificially the idea of culture and the habit of reading. In Britain one of the most pathetic of recent spectacles has been governments invoking the name of 'Education,' a parrot cry that becomes more meaningless the more we try to find out what it really means. It means, in practice, training in computers for the computer age, and very little else. The rest is just pious platitudes, and political football.

Where books are concerned – the novel in particular – in order to discover what the good is all about we must first have extensive experience of the bad. One of the most potent objections to the average university course in English is that students who have read little or nothing are confronted with 'the best', in selection, and have no idea – apart from the say-so of their teachers – why it is the best. There may be plenty of airport trash available, but in my experience its consumers are mainly middle-aged or elderly: the young have other things to do than to read books, even bad ones. By the time I was sixteen I had developed the habit of ingesting whatever books I came across, uncritically but also intensively, and most of them were very bad indeed (this was about the time when the first paperbacks were coming in, but had secured no big hold on the market – the books I read were mostly cheap reprints and old library copies). But books and stories were the world one lived in – a much more real world than the day-to-day one of mere living. This no doubt had its drawbacks, but it gave one something to do, at a time when the young were expected to amuse themselves. Kipling describes the phenomenon in his story 'Baa Baa Black Sheep'. The young boy reads everything he can get hold of, which is not much – a few now forgotten Victorian bestsellers – and then has nothing to do but to live the life suggested by his wonder at the books, which were of course intended for grown-up reading. He ponders the meaning of fascinating new incomprehensible words he has found, exchanges conversations with imaginary people, marches invisible armies up and down the stairs.

It's interesting to note that this other world is not only wonderful and detailed and comprehensive, but a purely external world that has nothing to do with the young reader at all. He merely wonders at it, feeds greedily on it. Of course Kipling later became a writer, and these early experiences must have contributed an enormous but invisible – indeed unconscious – fund to his ultimate performers as a writer. But they had nothing to do with himself, his young self as it was, and that was their great charm at the time: they constituted a new and intoxicating world. If such a world has never come into being for you, as a reader, the effect of reading a few books – and no doubt good books – a bit later on in life, probably when you are a student, is very different. It produces an interest, not in the books themselves, but in yourself. And at the same time the student is reading the texts for his course, he or she is very likely concerned too with a course on writing. Do it yourself – 'creative' writing. And yet of course in most cases it is hardly creative but self-creative, self-absorbing, self-proclaiming. Books as an aid to finding out who you really are.

This may have its advantages too, but it certainly does not encourage a true habit of reading. It is at this point that the mocking presence of Gore Vidal makes an appearance, pointing out that we have too many writers or would-be writers today, but all too few readers. Two few persons, that is, who regard books as another world, a world which has become as necessary to them as breathing. An addiction? Not really, for the invisible presence of such another world not only makes life itself far more interesting, but makes it more tolerable to live in the ordinary day-to-day one. Books are an escape, certainly; but for that reason they are also therapy for living. 'Escapism' used to be a derogatory term. When I was young it meant a reluctance to confront the stern realities of the real world, the political and social world. There is still plenty of escapism about, but it's seldom called that any more: the term has gone out of fashion. Harmless old-fashioned escapism has usually been replaced today by various sorts of addiction, some of them far from harmless.

It's quite difficult to remember now the social and temporal climate in which books, like knitting or singing round the piano, were the normal thing, even the drab usual daily thing, the thing everyone took for granted. In a quaint little compendium on 'What to Read and Why' the novelist Arnold Bennett took it for granted that everyone *read*, even read for a good number of hours a week. The question that exercised him was what was the best kind of thing to read; the thing that would make you feel modest pride if someone asked you what you had been doing the previous evening, and you were able to answer not just 'I was reading' –

that was normal – but 'I was reading such and such by so and so'. No TV in Bennett's day of course: even the radio (which in England was always known as 'the wireless') was a bit dodgy. So reading really was a necessity. Like knitting, and playing cards, and singing round the piano.

There is a delightful moment in Elizabeth Bowen's best-known novel, *The Death of the Heart*, of social life in a small seaside town in the thirties. One of the young women characters works in Boots' circulating library, a great feature of life in such places. Her job is regarded as a genteel one, suitable for a 'lady', because she has an underling of slightly inferior social status, who is paid actually to read the books and make suitable recommendations of them to customers, something beneath the dignity of the mildly dashing young woman who acts as a kind of 'front', welcoming the customers, and gossiping with them. It is clear that the author of the novel regards this arrangement as quite normal, but is amused by it, as she takes for granted her readers will be too. Indeed, and at this distance of time, we can see there are several quite subtle sociological points involved. Reading in those days was not, as it is today, a rather unusual occupation, nor was it found among a literate and superior social class. On the contrary, it conferred no social status at all: it was as 'democratic' as bingo is today. The girl who is paid to read the books, so that she can advise the customers, acquires no prestige from doing so – rather the opposite – and the young 'lady' who gives the library a social cachet does so because she is above the mere reading of books. Elizabeth Bowen regards this girl both with amusement and in a sense with a kind of admiration. Utterly addicted to and dependent upon books as she herself is, like all writers and readers, at least in those days, as a novelist she observes almost wistfully those few dashing spirits who can live without them. Such an accomplishment, and such independency, were in an age when people read books as continuously and unthinkingly as they smoked cigarettes.

To a book lover there is something slightly disquieting today about the way in which television has ingested not only the literary classics, from Jane Austen to *The Last of the Mohicans*, but the whole spectrum of reading matter. Not so much for its own immediate purposes as spectacle, but by a sort of divine right as top artistic medium, exercising an ultimate control over the circulation and popularity of the bookish world. Sales of Jane Austen notoriously shot up after the televising of *Pride and Prejudice* and

Persuasion; and many readers may have found – I experienced it myself – that their own private sense of the image and tone of these books had been affected, though we may hope not irreparably, by a purely visual imprint now imposed on the reading surface of the mind. Jane Austen's words and sentences, creating Elizabeth and Mr Darcy and the others, had been overprinted by their screen images, losing all their purely verbal subtlety in the process. Shakespeare is said to have been one of the first, if not *the* first, author to refer to the common daily phenomenon of a picture in the mind – 'in my mind's eye', as Hamlet says. That was where he thought he saw his dead father; and Wordsworth, seeing daffodils by a lakeside two hundred years later, 'fluttering and dancing in the breeze', found that an even greater pleasure than his original sight of them was to recall them – flashing 'on that inward eye/That is the bliss of solitude.' If we attempt visually to imagine Wordsworth's experience today we shall probably find ourselves 'remembering' some pastoral scene – perhaps an advertisement – beautifully created on the TV screen, now installed among our involuntary collection of associated memories as a piece of virtual reality.

The whole problem of technological and visual 'overlay' is a fascinating one, though it may be a painful one for the print addict and the bookworm, whose 'mind's eye', or 'inward eye', is trained on another kind of image than the visual. One of the most important freedoms of reading is the ability conferred on us by a good writer to recognise, know, and be entirely at home with his characters without actually seeing them 'in the mind's eye'. We know them by all sorts of subtle signs, hints, verbal indications, and these make us free of their creation and their personalities without confining us to our own mental pictures from life, or from a cathode-ray tube. Madame Bovary and Anna Karenina exist, and vividly exist, but not as visual images: the reading mind is free to explore and to understand them without seeing them. It is this freedom which is foreclosed by the TV screen, when it 'brings them to life' itself and – inevitably an ironical concept – by introducing them to us in the guise of actors and actresses. The producer's choice may have been felicitous: the actor or actress may seem just right for the part, but the 'part', once the prerogative and possession of the reader, has now become as public and as banal as any other media photograph: Anna Karenina as much on photographic show as Princess Diana.

Technology being what it is the process has been going on some time – the cinema began it a long time before television – and there is even an analogy with words and music: the words that have been arbitrarily added to a melody by Chopin, Elgar, or Holst have the unfortunate effect of overlaying the music, so that whenever it is played and heard in the head the words come too, irremediably intrusive, as if relayed on a monitor screen. Human memory has its own kinds of technology, delicately adjusted and disastrous to interfere with. Certainly the human technology of book reading, subtle and non-visual – except in complex and indefinable ways – cannot help but be insulted by a manufactured screen image from which there is ever afterwards no escape.

There seems to be a connection, too, between 'Vidal's Law', as one might refer to it – the desire, that is, to create and to write instead of to read – and the desire of the media to impose itself on authors like Jane Austen, and in doing so to make them an aspect of itself and its own world. Many novels today give the impression that they were not intended to be *read*, only to be *written*: a bizarre paradox, but one fully in keeping with the implications of 'Vidal's Law'. The further point of course is that they were intended not only to be written but to be filmed, and so 'viewed'. The author in creation saw them as if coming to life – their proper and destined life – on the TV screen.

That was certainly the impression I formed when serving in 1994 as chairman of the Booker Prize, an annual event in the British literary world, and one which is said to have made the reputations of several famous novelists who have won it, including Salman Rushdie. (Neither Martin Amis nor Julian Barnes, on the other hand, have managed to win it, or even appear on its shortlist.) My own reaction was to find most of the entries exceedingly hard to read, precisely because they seemed to have been written by someone determined to be a novelist, but well aware that few if any readers were going to read him. He or she was aware that the Booker jury consisted, as it were, of captive readers, who had no choice but to read the book in order to give the prize. But such authors made no concession to the idea that their duty as well as their best policy might be to think as they wrote what their readers might feel and respond to. Instead they were far too interested in themselves, and in being themselves in what they wrote. None of them won the prize, though there were brisk differences and disputes before we were finally able to come up with a winner of some sort; and even so one jury-woman left the meeting, declaring that the novel finally selected would only win over her dead body.

The rest of the jury managed to restrain her from performing the ultimate sacrifice, and the prize was duly awarded, although I can now hardly remember the name of the book, or why the jurywoman objected to it so strongly. It was obscene, certainly: the four-letter words being repeated on every page in a routine sort of way. But that was not what had bothered the jurywoman – of course not. Like everyone else who read novels now she was used to it, totally inured to it. Not like the Russian chair-woman of the first Russian Booker prize, which I had served on the previous year in Moscow. Russian readers are still quite unaccustomed to routine western-style obscenity in novels, even though contemporary Russian writers are now trying conscien-tiously to provide it, as a needful part of new fashion. The Russian chairwoman had said forcefully of one entry that it was the most disgusting book she had ever tried to read. I remembered now, as the next year's prize was being discussed in England, how surprised by that I and a fellow-juror on the Russian panel – an American woman – had been. From the same Russian novel, which we had both read, we couldn't see what the fuss was about. To us it seemed quite 'normal'.

But if that was not this English jurywoman's problem, then what was? The novel, which eventually and by a process of bargaining received the prize, had disturbed her deeply in some way – really upset her. That was clear. As I pondered the question it suddenly struck me that she must have felt herself exposed to the author of the book – almost as if violated by him. It was indeed a powerful and disturbing novel – that was, after all, why the jury had singled it out, and why they eventually awarded it the prize – and it had got to this jurywoman in some way that had repelled and even horrified her. She wanted nothing to do with it. I was fascinated by this reaction, not because I felt any-thing in the least like it myself, but because I saw that the author had indeed exposed himself to the jurywoman, sensitized her, appalled her. He had created a world – a world inside his own art – with which she wanted nothing to do. She had certainly responded passionately to the novel, but it was, so to speak, an inverted or reversed passion, a passion of abhorrence.

And yet this invention by the novelist of a world of his own – good or bad – is probably the crux of the matter. If we respond positively to his world we develop our own kind of passion for it: we become hooked. This situation has not changed. Realism, modernism, magic realism, post-modernism, many other fashions, have come and gone, as has so much of literary theory, but the creation of a world unlike any other still remains the one stable criterion where the novelist and his public are concerned. Could it be that this fact is connected with two things: 'Vidal's Law', if we give it that name, and a corresponding lack of interest today in novel reading and in the novel as a form? Could it perhaps be that the novelist today is failing to create a complete and satisfying world of his own, a world like that of Dickens or Dostoevsky or Tolkien or P. G. Wodehouse, a world that is instantly recognisable once the reader has got to know it, and perhaps come to develop his own kind of addiction?

If this is so, what is the explanation? It could prove to be a general impatience with invention itself, with make-believe; and a growing preference for fact, or at least for 'faction', in place of fiction. Has fiction today tended to become too fact-bound, too realistic, in spite of magic realism, or post-surrealism, or other varieties of fantasy? That seems possible. It may equally be true that Vidal's impression that everybody wants to write, nobody to read, diagnoses a self-defeating process. For it is impossible to create a novelist's world by DIY methods. However the process is accomplished it remains a mysterious one, which cannot either be taught or learned. A novelist's world can only be recognised when it has come into being, and the novelist himself is probably the last person who can fully explain how it comes about. Nor can such a world be imitated, except in the most superficial sense, or by the process of parody. One of the dire things about television versions of the classics is that they deprive the original of its true world, substituting one which only approximates it. This is so not only in the case of *Wuthering Heights* or *Pride and Prejudice*. The same thing happens with a modern classic, for example Anthony Powell's twelve-volume series, *A Dance to the Music of Time*. Like Proust's *Remembrance of Things Past*, of which it contains a conscious echo, Powell's masterpiece moves slowly and cumulatively, impressing the personality of its denizens upon the reader by degrees, until it becomes clear both that no world like this has ever existed or could exist, and that such a work of art can be, at the same time, a remarkably accurate social document.

In terms of TV, or in any other media than its own, this unique paradox of the *roman fleuve* is quite lost. Its slow motion has to be speeded up, and becomes unrecognisable; its jokes and inner references cease to make extended sense: the tortoise-like subtlety disappears. It is arguably a sign of weakness in the Powell series that this should be so: after all, *Hamlet* or *Henry V* or even Henry James survive exposure to the media pretty well, becoming for the duration of a film something different, but without any excessive sense of denaturing or loss. No doubt they represent art of another kind, art that is less dependent on a unique and specialized world of its own. However that may be it is of interest for our purposes to look in conclusion at what Powell as an artist has had to say himself about the way a novel or series of novels, like his own, comes to be written. In the concluding volume, *Hearing Secret Harmonies*, he fabricates a brief dialogue between his own novelist narrator, and another highly opinionated writer of novels and stories, bearing the wonder name of X. Trapnell.

'People think because a novel's invented,' claims Trapnell, 'that it isn't true. Exactly the reverse is the case ... The biographer, even at his best, can only be tentative, empirical. The autobiographer, for his part, is imprisoned in his own egotism ... In contrast with the other two, the novelist is a god, creating his man, making him breathe and walk. The man, created in his own image, provides information about the god.' The narrator-author agrees, though with a few reservations, remarking elsewhere in the series, but again through the medium of his invented novelist Trapnell, that 'a writer writes what he is'.

The successful novelist, in fact, creates a world which supplies a total fund of information about its creator. He cannot help writing 'what he is'. Powell's remarks on autobiography show us, on the other hand, why the would-be novelist who desires to write in order to 'be himself' – to find out who he is or to create himself – cannot but be a failure as a novelist. Instead of becoming a god, and creating a world which in the process of creation reveals who he is, he has done no more than contribute some inevitably dubious and misleading data towards his own biography. And that is not the same thing at all. Or, indeed, the right thing to do for a novelist. The conclusion, even if perhaps an over-simple one, is that to write about oneself is a certain recipe for false-ness, as well as, in general, for bad writing, whereas to create in art a world of one's own is to reveal oneself fully and accurately, though involuntarily, to the reader. And the second, indirect, process is the one that holds the truest literary fascination for an addicted reader.

As it happens, my own family could be said to afford a kind of case-history of the process. My wife Iris Murdoch, a well-known novelist, has certainly constructed over the years a body of work – twenty-seven or so masterpieces of fiction – which are imme- diately recognizable by their readers as having created a unique world of the imagination. I have often heard people say 'It was rather an Iris Murdoch situation' or (of an acquaintance) 'she's very much an Iris Murdoch character'. Readers and fans know at once, through the operation of a kind of mutual mental computer, just what sort of person or situation is being referred to. These persons and situations are also herself, Iris Murdoch, in that they disclose the inner workings, passions and compulsions of her own mind. None of them appears on the surface of our daily life; but I, like all her readers, have come to recognise and to love the depth and inwardness of her spirit and personality, revealed in her novels.

My own case is, to put it mildly, somewhat different. I am a teacher and critic by trade, having become both by a stroke of luck when I was about twenty-eight years old. At the time I had written a single, and youthful, novel prompted to the undertak- ing by my professor's wife, a kindly soul who once enquired whether I had ever written one, or proposed to write one. I answered yes, which was untrue: I had never considered the matter at all. But now I felt obliged to try, so I turned to and in four months produced a workmanlike job, mostly about my time in the army during and after the war. When published it turned out to be moderately successful, and was certainly no worse, if not greatly better, than the general run of fiction I had to read, many years later, for the Booker Prize. The point of interest is that I had joined, if inadvertently, the Gore Vidal awkward squad: those who want not to read but to write; and in so doing I was not writing as myself, the person I really was, but had invented a persona and a situation which made an excuse for putting pen to paper. Like most novels it was a fraud, even though one I had enjoyed pulling off.

I got married about this time, and perceiving my wife had true talent and more, I enjoyed providing a kind of friendly and critical receptor, which she could use to test her own imagination, and the reality of her writing self. I found my own proper *métier* in the meantime, and I wrote critical books based on my teaching experience. As a relaxation in retirement I have written some more novels. I enjoy doing them, and friends say they are quite a pleasure to read, but they offer no unique and original world for a reader to explore and inhabit. That is the rarest of achievements, but the only worth-while sign of a true novelist. The writer who can do it, and who has done it, will always find a passionate reader.

3

Casaubon's Syndrome, or Reader Rampant

FERDINAND MOUNT

The dust jacket was green and grey, divided diagonally, I think. There was nothing to attract my attention about the book's exterior – chaste, not to say pallid, no picture on it – nothing except the title, which suggested that it might have strayed from the children's shelf upstairs. I read it through almost without stopping, alternately enthralled by the heroism and disgusted by the treachery of the characters. I taught my sister the verses of the song, because she was still too young to read (I was six and she must then have been four). Neither of us could sing in tune, then, or now, but we belted out the words remorselessly, day after day, to what we imagined to be the tune of Clementine, just as the book prescribed:

> Beasts of England, beasts of Ireland,
> Beasts of every land and clime,
> Harken to my joyful tidings
> Of the golden future time.

I was amazed, and a little aggrieved, later on to be told that the book was an allegory of some sort, too complicated to be explained to me in one go. It was perfect just as it was, with no subtext. My aunt and uncle, Violet and Tony Powell, were close friends of George Orwell, and she reported to him how I had read *Animal Farm* with such delight. Orwell was delighted too. I was the best of all possible evidence that he had succeeded in writing clear prose which spoke straight to the reader.

As the years passed, however, after this precocious start, I turned out to be one of those extreme cases Orwell might not have approved of so much: someone who tended to regard books as more real than life, more reliable, more concrete even. As so often, precocity had grown into something even more repulsive: the bibliomaniac's cold carapace that repels ordinary experience. And by books I mean books, not words. *Les Mots* – so talismanic for chatterboxes like Sartre – seemed to me shadowy, fleeting things, until after they were safely sunk into the page, their hooks and uprights and downstrokes absorbed in that thick, breadlike paper that pre-war novels were printed on.

Speech, conversation, verbal instruction – all these seemed to me then, and sometimes still seem, imperfect, transitional substitutes for the real thing, that higher mode of communication which was so neatly sandwiched between cloth boards and which did indeed, when assembled in sufficient numbers, furnish a room with their agreeable miscellany of size, colour and pattern. This is a discreditable kind of deviance, I am aware of that: Casaubon's Syndrome. It is a thinblooded, less than fully human lifestyle – a denial of Life, in the sense so obscurely bruited by that obsessive bookman, F. R. Leavis. If exposed too rawly, it can offend, even shock. I once declared that I had read so much about Elizabeth Taylor that actually having an affair with her wouldn't add much. This bewildered the old friends whom I was talking to (quite bookish people themselves); for years afterwards, they referred to my declaration with a mixture of derision and disbelief. It is, I suppose the bookman's version of Plato's cave, lived experience a mere shadow-show against the eternal reality of books. I can still remember, at roughly the age I read *Animal Farm*, the first thrill of the thought that books lived longer than the people who had written them.

To describe all this as 'a passion for reading' is an understatement; it doesn't begin to do justice to the indifference to the outside world which keeps the bookman's head still buried in the guide book while he is standing on the edge of the Grand Canyon or the steps of Salisbury Cathedral. Nor is it to be confused with a passion for books as objects. I certainly grow fond of books I have known all my life. To come upon a book in my own shelves that was on my parents' shelves forty years ago sometimes makes the heart stop: the dove-grey binding of David Cecil's *Stricken Deer* (his life of Cowper, in which, for once, all Cecil's sensibility and charm reach the page); the brown-and-red-speckled Chapman & Hall editions of Evelyn Waugh, with lurking among them the smaller dirty-pink copy of *Brideshead Revisited*, inscribed to my mother 'with love from Evelyn,' a proud possession, although we all pretended not to like the book when we were at university because we were against sentimentality; the orange-and-white scrolls and fleur-de-lis of Tancred Borenius's *Florentine Frescoes*, the first book which drew me to Italian painting; the Herbert Jenkins Pegasus on the P. G. Wodehouses (having only a hazy idea of publishing and knowing no other books from that firm, I imagined that Herbert Jenkins was some kind of associate of Wodehouse's, perhaps now and then allowed to write some of the more pedestrian passages); the three dark-blue volumes of Carlyle's *French Revolution*; the maroon backs of the pocket Conrads, with their tingling one-word titles – *Youth, Victory, Nostromo* – and, even then sounding a little outrageous, *The Nigger of the Narcissus*; the three volumes of Osbert Sitwell's autobiography, conveying one into a world of mad, unhappy extravagance, and the rather dingier backs of the L. P. Hartleys, in particular that mysterious work *The Shrimp and the Anem one* (the hyphen on the spine had faded). Then there were the old rose-pink Thackerays – apart from *Vanity Fair*, I only read the humorous sketches and wondered why he was considered a grown-up writer.

Fine bindings meant little to me. My father picked up a handsome set of Swift cheap, but these were latecomers to the shrine, and I felt no special urge to tackle them. There was a kind of fetishism at work here. New books coming into the house (largely as monthly selections from the Book Society) seemed to me inferior products, arriving as they did with the rest of the mail, not having achieved the sacrosanct status of being part of a Library. This shelf snobbery was not wholly misplaced. One or two of the Book Society books have achieved an enduring reputation – Patrick Leigh Fermor's *The Violins of St. Jacques*, for example – but many of the others, by authors like Rumer Godden, John Masters and R. C. Hutchinson (still going long after the war), have faded into that gentle obscurity which overtakes middlebrow bestsellers. All of them seemed unreadable to me then, but not because of any precocious critical discrimination; I suspected them of being trumpery stuff before I had read a word, partly because the subscription to the Book Society was a generous Christmas present from my uncle Frank, who was thought to have no literary taste.

But then nor did I. Charming lightweight authors like E. M. Delafield – *Thank Heaven Fasting, What is Love?, Diary of a Provincial Lady* – were read with pleasure if they had served their time on the shelf. The colonel's wife from next door found me engrossed in *Thank Heaven Fasting* when I was supposed to be watching a cricket match; she read a few pages and tossed it back to me with disdain, saying 'That's not boys' stuff,' intimating that I ought to be out in the middle facing the fast bowling. It was too awkward to explain that, in fact, I was quite fond of cricket and also enjoyed rugged adventure stories, from Henty to Bulldog Drummond (James Bond not yet having arrived on the scene), but, as is the case with most passionate readers in early life, my tastes were indiscriminate and omnivorous, extending far beyond books to take in any printed matter to hand, from the wording on cereal packets and sauce bottles to the small print on a bus ticket or a railway by-law. The notion that your choice in books might define you as a person, just like your choice in clothes or records, was alien to me. I was no more inclined to restrict myself to any particular *type* of reading matter, to a genre of novel, or to books sharing a single political or philosophical world-view – than I could prevent (or wish to prevent) my eyes from taking in unwelcome sights and unpleasant people.

It is this last and central aspect of the true passion for reading – its all-devouring, world-of-its-own nature – that brings it into conflict with those who do not share the passion, and also brings it within range of the big guns of modern literary theory. A passion for books as sacred objects, intimately bound up with memories of home and childhood, is a lesser passion that might be felt for any such domains of early pleasure: the garden, the pictures on the wall, one's first favourite radio programmes or cinema outings, memories of sporting occasions watched or taken part in, services in church or synagogue. Again, a passion for a particular type of reading matter may be an extension of or a prelude to a desired kind of life, at first only vaguely dreamed of but then taking a firmer outline and leading on to practical decisions: a predilection for sea stories leading on to an enthusiasm for sailing and eventually to a life at sea. Reading in this sense is an accessory to life, and an influence which could just as well have been exercised through some other medium, such as film.

But the true reading passion goes deeper and wider, leaving its victim convinced that knowledge and experience are most vividly, most reliably, most lastingly transmitted through the printed page. This applies equally to technical books that explain how to make a soufflé, tie a knot or sail a boat as to works of the imagination – poetry, fiction or philosophy. The setting of words on the page provides an opportunity that no other medium offers for the author to collect his own thoughts, uncontaminated by outside babble, and put them down in enduring, unchanging form; for his part, the reader then picks up these thoughts, equally uncontaminated by the outside world, and imbibes, appreciates, and eventually stores them away for good – in both the temporal and moral sense. No word is spoken during the encounter; it is silent and exclusive. (Although it is argued that silent reading, without moving one's lips, is quite a recent invention, I'm not sure how much difference this makes to the reader–author relationship.) One could say that the transmission is like that of a computer free of viruses, but that would be to demean the event, and also to misrepresent it. For the whole point of the encounter between the reader and the author, as understood by the passionate reader, is that it is an encounter between two responsible *agents*. Each of us knows what he is trying to do. This does not necessarily mean that either of us does it perfectly. A bad author may be clumsy or sentimental; he may organize his material badly or leave out the wrong things. All the same, he has certain aims in view, and if he fails to achieve them, that is because he lacks the requisite talent or has not worked hard or long enough. There is no inherent complication in the task, no outside force spoiling his aim. The same goes for the reader; we may fail to understand something through inattention or stupidity; if we get stuck in a book, it may be our fault, or it may be the author's. But the medium sets no inherent obstacles to our full understanding or enjoyment. And on the whole, we like to think that we usually 'get the best' out of a book; or if we don't, if we continue to be baffled, bored or annoyed, we toss the book aside and try something else.

Now all these assumptions are denied or undermined by the prevailing masters of modern literary theory (I shall not bother to differentiate them, partly because I am not equipped to do so, and partly because the central line of criticism seems to be common to most of them). The postmodernist masters argue that any simple relationship between the author and 'his' text is an illusion; each is a mass of influences, some half-digested, some more or less unconscious. It is wrong to speak of either originality or intention as belonging to an author; a text simply issues at a particular moment, and its career only begins there, for each fresh reading alters it in subtle and ever-thickening ways, so that even if an author had something which could be dignified by the name of *final* intention, that intention would not, could not be honoured by the reader. It is as true of texts as of everything else in life that everything flows, nothing stays. Our pleasure in books is like that of dabbling one's fingers in the water, the 'same' water that flowed past the author miles upstream but now flows on past us, discoloured by different weeds and algae and with different fish flashing through it, and so not the same in any meaningful sense.

It is an intoxicating, disorienting theory, which also provides a convenient retirement home for disillusioned Marxists. The bourgeoisie, so cruelly triumphant in the world of affairs, can still be harried and teased and disabused of their false consciousness in the domain of literature.

The implications of theory are also infinitely regressive. If we cannot speak of what Wordsworth meant, how can we speak of what Derrida means? Indeed, what continuity or identity is there to be found in the world? If 'Kubla Khan' now is not the 'Kubla Khan' the person from Porlock interrupted, then nor is the apple I bought yesterday the same apple today. Nor, for all the talk of difference, does there seem to be much differentiating to be done in the deconstruction of texts. If every work is really only part of the endless flow of intertextuality, how can we establish whether some works are more intertextual than others, that is, less original? If everything is derived, we can no longer identify any particular work as derivative. The critic seems inexorably driven to abolish his own function, which is to discriminate. Indeed, this flight from the comparative cripples the critic in almost all his work. For example: the text of Shakespeare is unstable (because of pirates and bad copyists and the compressions and distortions of stage production), but if we deduce from this that all texts must be unstable, then we lose the ability to notice that some texts are more stable, *much* more stable, than others.

Yet is the author–text–reader relationship really this undifferentiated flow of stuff? One cannot ignore the fact that there is a human being at either end of it, a separate individual. What distinguishes a responsible agent is *not* that he is wholly free of the influence of others (has such a person ever existed? Could such a person exist and make himself understood?) but, more simply and less ambitiously, that he is capable of exercising a judgement or playing a role that is unambiguously his. He may do this well or badly; he may fulfil our hopes or execute our commands, or he may fail to or refuse to, but we recognize that it is up to him and that, even though he may have been indoctrinated by the Jesuits or the U.S. Marine Corps, we cannot guarantee that he will obey us; nor can we guarantee to predict his actions and reactions. Now that is what a writer is like, even a dull obedient hack; that is what a reader is like too, even one who always reads thrillers or Mills & Boon romances. One may read or write under all sorts of outside influences; one may be ordered to read or write something by one's church or political party. But one may also refuse and rebel; one may be froward or recusant. And because the act of reading is so private, even when carrying out the command, as a reader one can keep one's true thoughts to oneself. And once these powers – of open rebellion or of silent dissent – are acknowledged, it is difficult to deny the reality of the independent will at work. We do not need to prove here that the will is even partially free, we need only to note the plain fact of independence. To identify someone as a responsible agent, it is sufficient only to show that he possesses the capacity to disobey instructions. What chain of influences may have ultimately led to any particular act of disobedience is not for us to track down.

As one reads modern critical theory in all its variants and subvariants, one begins to feel that its analysis is not so much empty as the wrong way round. Far from being caught up in a process over which they have no control, both the writer and the reader are conspicuously wilful, intention-rich beings. Even in our imitations of others, whether conscious or unconscious, there is something which is our own, a muscular core of selfhood which we feel clenching up inside ourselves and preparing to defend its integrity even in such banal judgements as 'Well, I didn't really like the book much. The girl just wasn't convincing.'

True, we do not understand Shakespeare as the contemporary readers of the First Folio understood him. For one thing, we simply find him much more difficult; the syntax is too complex, some of the words are obsolete or obscure, many more have changed their meaning. It would be absurd, though, to say therefore that we read him differently; we just don't read him so well, just as we do not read German quite as well as the Germans, even if we have a working knowledge of the language.

In this respect, reading is much the same as listening. We may mishear, because the speaker's voice is too indistinct, or his brogue is too thick. Or we may misunderstand, because his vocabulary is too abstruse or laced with dialect words, because his words are interspersed with so much superfluous verbiage, or because we mistake his emphasis. Or we may fail to understand, because we are too ignorant, or too humourless. But most of the time, we reckon we understand well enough for our purposes; we do not in ordinary life despair of the possibility of communicating effectively with others. But to say that we understand the message is not to claim that we understand the speaker, any more than we would claim to understand the innermost feelings of our fellow motorists merely because we have a working understanding of their motoring manoeuvres.

But reading is an improvement on listening, since it has built-in arrangements for speed variation and playback. We can read quickly to get the gist, or as slowly as we like, savouring each word; we can reread the page we have just read, or go back to the first chapter to remind ourselves of where we started, or skip forward to the end to see whether our interpretation of the direction of the text is a correct one. With speech, these possibilities are available less often, and likely to be called on mostly in such cases as that of a group of detectives playing and replaying the tape of a ransom demand, that is to say, in cases of extreme importance, matters sometimes of life and death.

True, there are other ways in which the passage of time has made Shakespeare more difficult for us. Key concepts in some of the plays don't mean so much to us, the divine anointment of kings, for example. To enter into *Richard II* properly, we will need to make an effort of the imagination. If we don't manage it, if the whole premise of the play thereby comes to seem baffling or a little silly, then I would prefer to say that we had not got the hang of the play, rather than that we were reading it 'differently'. A translation or a stage production of Chekhov that blurs the irony or exaggerates the sentimentality is simply mistaken; so is an excessively religiose interpretation of Kafka. Indeed, it is the critic's task to show us why the people who make these mistakes are mistaken.

Well then, what about cases where we understand something in the book that the author himself simply doesn't understand, where coming a century or two later, we are several steps ahead of him? Some theme or some quirk of character that he takes for granted as part of the human condition we see as conditioned by the assumptions of his time – assumptions about class or colonialism or gender, say.

At first sight, such cases may seem to license us to talk of 'reading' the book differently from the author (and his contemporaries). But if you turn to comparable cases where there is no time-lag between the writing and the reading – say, the treatment of women in the novels of Kingsley and Martin Amis – I don't think a hostile feminist would naturally say that she read the novels differently from the authors; she would simply say 'the Amises are benighted male chauvinists who hate women and don't treat them as full human beings.' The critic who dislikes the treatment of women in those books, or in Lawrence or Hemingway, or in *The Taming of the Shrew*, is *arguing with* the author – which is what critics are partly for. She is not transmuting the text into a different text. Exegesis is not alchemy.

Critical theorists, I think, tend to over-sensualize the reader's encounter with the text. They see the two parties as locked in lascivious embrace, from which the text emerges so stained and rumpled that its author wouldn't recognize it, while the reader stumbles away, his senses transported, his faculties drained. In this passionate grappling, there is no space for disengaged appreciation.

But is this really how we read? Even when we are passionately absorbed by a book, there is a part of our mind which remains reserved for detached judgement and which may be switched on at any time. And it is part of the pleasure that the author may, so to speak, appeal over the head of the absorbed, passionate part to tickle the drier fancy. He may speak directly to Gentle Reader, in facetious or sorrowful lament over the state of the world or the behaviour of his characters. The unreliable narrator, the flashbacks and flashforwards, and all the other ancient author's tricks which are said to 'subvert' the text could also be described as part of a conversation between the writer and the reader *about* the book. As with any conversation, there are hazards. One participant may be quicker than the other. If it is the author who is the quicker-witted, he may be playing with the reader, deluging him with echoes and allusions he is too slow to catch, teasing his prejudices, parodying his favourite genres, or parodying the parody. On the other hand, the author may be genuinely appealing for sympathy, reaching out to a fellow-creature, helping him, in

Dr Johnson's formulation, to endure life as well as to enjoy it. Sometimes the author may be attempting both approaches at once. When Sterne assured his bookseller Thomas Becket that *A Sentimental Journey* is 'an original work and likely to take in all kinds of Readers – the proof of the pudding is in the eating', he surely means 'take in' both in the sense of 'cater for' and in the sense of 'fool', for the book appealed instantly to sentimentalists and cynics alike – and to postmodernist critics too, who admire the way Sterne 'subverts' the romantic genre. Here the postmodernists are at one with Johnson, who called the vivacious Mary Monckton a dunce because she insisted that some of Sterne's writings were 'very pathetic'. But Johnson and the postmodernists are only half-right: they see the irony where poor Mary doesn't, but the pathetic and the poetic are there too – just as they are in the Gertie McDowell scene in *Ulysses*. Joyce, like Sterne, wants to have it both ways and is quite happy for us to have it both ways too. Like many literary types of ambiguity, these are both-and cases, rather than either-or, and deliberately so.

And, of course, some literary tricks work only if the reader *is* fooled. At the end of Agatha Christie's *Murder of Roger Ackroyd*, when the narrator reveals himself to be the murderer, the deceived reader can only ruefully acknowledge that he has been beautifully had. In other cases, where the writer breaks off now and then to discourse, as Balzac will on human psychology or the workings of capitalism, or as Tolstoy does on the working of history, we may be profoundly irritated and wish to tell the author to get on with it, but if he won't, we can always skip, just as one may stop listening to someone until he says something that interests us.

And even when the detachment that we retain in the midst of the engagement presses us further – not merely to argue with the author but to *see through* him – I am still reluctant to speak of reading the text differently. For one thing, if we can truthfully claim to be seeing through the assumptions which he shared with his contemporaries and which we no longer share, we must first have a competent understanding of those assumptions, about the position of women in Jane Austen, say, or the importance of the Empire in Kipling. And with many such words, modern critics often fail to acknowledge or to grasp just how far it is the author himself who helps us to understand those assumptions. Kipling and Jane Austen, for example, are fully aware of their themes, make them quite explicit, and we can pursue the implications of those themes through all the words and actions of their characters. The lack of employment prospects for women, the importance of making a good match, or the need to do one's duty and keep a stiff upper lip – such assumptions may disgust us, but in 'foregrounding' them, we are not introducing elements which are not in the text. And if we do introduce elements which exist only in our own minds and are not securely grounded in the text, then we are likely to be misreading. We must read through the book properly first, in the terms the author intended, before we can claim to see through it.

But why break off from our amble round the shelves to labour these points? What has the agreeable browsing of the bookman to do with the menacing abstractions of the critical theorist? Because, I think, the delusions of critical theory derive ultimately from the bookman's apparently harmless life, for the bookman is not simply an inoffensive collector. He is different from other hobbyists. The keen philatelist, for example, does not believe that by collecting the stamps of Mongolia rather than Morocco he is affecting the destiny of those countries: the pigeon fancier does not imagine that he has mastered the mysteries of flight; but the obsessive bookman in his blissful solitude does begin to believe something comparable. He begins to perceive himself as the thinking, feeling centre of the universe; no other judgement matters except his own; the text has not reached its true destination, has not really *lived* until it has reached his eyes. By comparison, the author dissolves into mere cipher, tosses in his little cockleshell of conceit upon the huge waves of his epoch, barely conscious of what he is doing – and not doing it alone, as often as not. The theorist seizes with delight upon the occasions (few enough, in all conscience) in which posterity has failed to notice the contribution of the author's helper – his wife, his editor, his sister. Did not Harriet Taylor write the important bits of John Stuart Mill? And Zelda provide the creative juice for Scott? And Ted Hughes steal from Sylvia Plath? And as for Dorothy and William Wordsworth. . . ?

Until recently, none of this was publicly recognized. The author sat up there smirking, enjoying his undeserved eminence. But now, we are told, the reader's day has arrived; he is flexing his muscles and preparing for power. It is at last being recognized that, coming later in time, the reader simply knows more. Like the scientist in the mock-humble metaphors of Bertrand de Chartres and Sir Francis Bacon, he may be a dwarf, but he is a dwarf seated on the shoulders of a giant, a sophisticated smartass of a dwarf. There is a curious agreement between otherwise warring factions, between say Leavisites and Derrideans, that reading is *the* art, indeed that all art ends by dissolving into reading.

In his classic study *Nationalism*, Elie Kedourie describes how the new revolutionary nationalist movements thrilled passionate young men in the early nineteenth century:

> Literature and philosophy gave entrance to a nobler, truer world, a world more real and more exciting than the actual world; and gradually the boundary between the world of imagination and the world of reality became blurred, and sometimes disappeared altogether. What was sometimes possible in books ought to be possible in reality. The reading of books became a political, a revolutionary activity. Thus, many a young man found himself advancing from the composition of poems to the manufacture of infernal machines; thus, in the intoxication of a poetic dream, Adam Mickiewicz found himself imploring God to bring about universal war in which Poland might once again secure independence. Politics could indeed be exciting, as exciting as the wonderful speculations of Schelling and Fichte. Mean provincial towns where nothing ever happens, dusty libraries, prosaic lecture-rooms became the stage of an absorbing secret game, a game of hide-and-seek, in which nothing was as it seemed, and everything took on the glowing colours of romance.

Over the last century and a half with the perversion and eventual reversal of so many revolutions that kind of glow has faded, those intoxicating draughts have grown stale and bitter. In their place has come an even more startling leap of the imagination. The reader now becomes World Master *without having to leave his chair*. In the world of virtual reality, the bibliomane is king. While the computer nerd chatters to his fellow global villagers, he, no longer Gentle Reader, but Reader Rampant, Lector Imperator Maximus, reforms the universe.

Alas, it is all a fantasy, just as it was to turn out a fantasy for the young revolutionaries who crashed into the rocks of reality in 1848. In reality, the text still sits there, a little blurred and chipped by the erosions and vandalisms of time perhaps, but still incised, unalterable. Meanwhile, the author lies prone, gigantic, motionless, apparently defunct. The dwarfs swarm all over him, trying to tie him down, once and for all, with their little nets and hooks, firing their critical staple-guns at his vulnerable points, but to no avail. The giant yawns, stretches himself, and the tiny threads snap and the staples fly away. We reread *King Lear*, or *The Prelude*, or *Bleak House* and forget the rest.

4

Books in My Life

G. THOMAS TANSELLE

As far back as I can remember, I was aware of the mahogany bookcases, lined with matched sets of volumes, that nearly filled the north wall of the living room of the house where I grew up. They are in fact still there, a dominating presence through four generations, ever since my grandfather – long before I was born – brought them home. He frequently surprised my grandmother with pieces of furniture (like the large cherry silver-chest on a matching table), or sets of Bavarian and Limoges china, or porcelain vases, or cut-glass bowls, sometimes antique and sometimes not; and, surrounded by these objects from infancy, I came to feel (before I could have expressed it) an aesthetic pleasure in being in touch with tangible testimony from the past. The bookcases were the kind, often called 'lawyers' bookcases,' that consisted of separate stackable shelves with glass doors; such bookcases, in the classic design of the Globe-Wernicke Company, were popular in the early years of the century, though the mahogany ones were always uncommon (ours – after many polishings – were totally black). There were sixteen shelves, four stacks of four, and they, with their green and red and dark blue contents, always attracted the immediate attention of anyone entering the room, through the archway near the opposite end, almost thirty feet away.

The books were not important or valuable editions, and the authors ranged widely – sets of Dickens, Thackeray, Dumas, and Irving were there, but so were the complete works of F. Marion Crawford and E. P. Roe. The contents, however, were perhaps less significant to me as a child than the palpable sense of authors' oeuvres, unmistakably conveyed by these multi-volume sets, and the solidity of literature as an element of our environment, which was proclaimed by the whole display. There were books elsewhere in the house as well: the upper hall, for instance, really a large squarish room filled with light from a broad window on the landing where the stairway turned, was furnished with the same style of glass-doored shelves (a few of these with leaded panes), which contained – among other books – some of the volumes that one of my aunts had acquired during her Sorbonne days in the early 1920s. I thus learned early that French books have a different look from American ones. What role all these books, arrayed prominently, indeed unavoidably, on both floors of the house, had on my life is not easy to say, but I am convinced it was important, even fundamental. That I became a literature scholar and professor probably stems more from another influence, the presence of teachers in my family (two aunts, an uncle, a great-aunt). But my also becoming a voracious book collector, an en-thusiastic admirer of books as physical objects, undoubtedly owes much to growing up in a space where the physicality of books insistently declared itself to me dozens of times every day. If any one object serves for me as a Proustian madeleine, it is probably those sectional glass-doored bookcases.

Most people, I believe, when coming across a title like the one I have given to this essay, would assume that the piece deals with reading and with the role, in the author's development, of the ideas encountered in the texts of books. Some other people, a far smaller group who regard themselves as collectors, might consider the possibility that the essay recounts the author's experiences in searching out and assembling a collection of physical objects. The idea that 'readers' and 'collectors' are fundamen-tally distinct in their approach to books is so widespread that very few people would think that both reading and collecting might be the dual concern here. Yet I could not write about my life with books unless I commented on the two together – and not simply as two activities that I happened to be engaged in but as inextricable pursuits. I have spent a good part of my pro-fessional life writing books and essays and delivering lectures that attempt to explain the connections between verbal works and their physical embodiments. But those connections should not for that reason be a more influential part of my life story than of any other booklover's history. That my attention to them does make my story atypical shows how far we still are, as a literate public, from understanding the nature of reading matter.

A comment once made by Aldous Huxley epitomizes the feelings that readers often display toward collectors. In the January 1920 number of the *London Mercury* (to which, in its early months, he regularly contributed a 'Bibliographical Notes and News' column), Huxley wrote, 'There are moments when one's literary sense gets the better of one's purely bibliographical instincts – moments when a profound irritation seizes one that people should be so stupid as to collect books because they are rare and not because they are worth reading.' I should say, in return, that one is constantly amazed at how an intelligent person like Huxley can repeat such a stupid thought. But the fact is that many otherwise intelligent people, who are able to think clearly about other kinds of artefacts, seem to have difficulty making sense of objects conveying verbal texts, such as books and manuscripts. They apparently believe that the texts can simply be plucked from the objects containing them and that the containers are irrelevant to the process of using the contents – indeed, that other containers would do as well. Yet everyone understands that to extract meaning from a nonverbal artefact one must examine all its physical details with care; and somehow the presence of a text dazzles people into assuming that the orderly procession of the words, line after line, has not been affected by the packaging and that books are one category of artefact in which it is not necessary to examine all the physical evidence.

The underlying problem, of course, is the difficulty of saying where a work of language exists. But if we can at least say that it exists wherever it is being read or recited, no matter in how many thousands of places simultaneously, then we know it is not tied to the object we hold in our hands in the same way that a painting is. Although this is the fact that leads people to treat the physical details of verbal objects as unimportant (and to believe that photocopies and digitized texts are as good as the originals), it actually supports the opposite position – for if we rely on objects as our primary witnesses for verbal works, then we had better be sure we have examined all the evidence they offer for evaluating the particular texts they report. Bibliographical scholars have been showing, for well over a century, the ways in which texts are affected by their journey through the printing and publishing process and the ways in which books bear clues to provide evidence for some of those alterations. If these clues are generally hidden and require searching out, there are other physical features, meant to be noticed, that also affect reading: the details

of book design convey information about how the producers of
books (sometimes including authors) wanted the texts to be perceived, and those details always do influence readers' responses,
whether in the intended way or not. But these are points I have
written about extensively over the years, and I shall not belabor
them here.

I hope, however, that they suggest why Huxley and people
like him are wrong not to connect reading with the physical book.
And they lead me to add a comment that would further infuri-
ate Huxley: I wish even more people would collect books that
are not 'worth reading.' His remark suggests that rarity and read-
ability are contrasting concepts, when in fact the 'rare' books that
are usually collected achieve their desirability precisely because
they are 'worth reading.' If more attention were paid to books
not of interest for their content (which can only mean 'not currently
of interest' because interests continually change), then more
physical evidence would be preserved – evidence that forms part
of the context for assessing the evidence in other books from the
same period. There is no book – or, indeed, any other object –
that is not worth saving for what it tells us of the past. I recently
wrote an essay for *Studies in Bibliography* entitled 'A Rationale of
Collecting,' in which I made the point that no collection of objects
is trivial, either on a personal level (its meaning in the life of the
person who assembled it) or in terms of its role in the advancement
of learning. Collecting, far from being a philistine or unintellectual
endeavor (as comments like Huxley's suggest), is fundamental
to the human pursuit of knowledge and self-understanding.

In that essay I decided that all kinds of collections, including
the seemingly casual accumulations that everyone has, must be
considered part of the same phenomenon, for all function similarly in the lives of their possessors. Everyone is a collector because
everyone feels the need to create a comprehensible personal
environment extracted from the chaos of the external world. One's
accumulated possessions, even when they seem disordered and
random, are linked by their connection with the same personality and by their role in making one feel that to some extent,
however small, the alien has been domesticated, the intractable
subjugated. This search for order impels some individuals to form
systematic collections as part of their total accumulations and causes
others to become scientists or scholars or artists. But they all share
the experience of creating their own physical surroundings, which

gives them a sense of control that influences the way they see the untamed wildness outside their private domains. And one person's assemblage of objects, being part of the external world faced by other people, inevitably affects the thinking of those other people. Collections are the basis for a great deal of what we call knowledge by causing us to see things differently: rearranged objects can in themselves provide revelations, or they can prepare us for making discoveries elsewhere – experiences then enshrined, for others to encounter, in essays or scientific papers or poems or paintings or further collections.

That collecting serves a social good adds to its pleasures for some people; for others the private enjoyments, which follow from satisfying a basic need, are enough. But in either case the personal and the public benefits are there, and intertwined. For that reason it is hard to make the distinction, which people often attempt to do, between a 'working library' and a 'book collection,' or between any other group of objects assembled for use and one brought together for aesthetic enjoyment. These boundaries are never distinct, and if need is taken – as it must be – to comprehend emotional as well as physical and professional requirements, they vanish altogether. There is a wholeness to individuals' possessions, whether they think there is or not. But what underlies this wholeness in each instance is a unique story, one out of an infinity of possible combinations of temperament, circumstance, and experience. Such histories are always of interest as variations on the theme of how the search for order is conducted, how self-definition is achieved.

My own story, whatever else it illustrates, offers an example of the way in which books bought as 'research tools' and those acquired as 'collector's items' refuse to stay within those categories. All my other possessions are of course relevant parts of the total picture: the bookcases in my Manhattan apartment (just like my grandfather's, except these are oak), the crystal paperweights on my Connecticut aunt's fold-down desk, the copper-lined tobacco stand, the paintings by E. E. Cummings, the Eskimo soapstone carvings, the Art Young cartoon, the Will Bradley posters, the eighteenth-century brass candlesticks, the Art Deco desk of my Illinois aunt, the mahogany pedestals from the family house, the nineteenth-century cane-bottomed dining-table chairs from my uncle's beach cottage, the black and gold side-chairs made from trees destroyed in the 1938 New England hurricane, the Indiana

limestone polyhedron on my writing table, and on and on – objects
greatly varying in their monetary value, inherited from friends
and relatives or purchased at many times and places, in many
moods. All these objects bring the past, and my past, into the
present, into my presence; like everyone else, I live surrounded
by a personal and an impersonal past. But the objects that dominate
my rooms, filling most walls and surfaces, many corners and
closet shelves, are books. And it is the books I wish to concentrate
on here.

Why books should dominate is perhaps the effect of those
imposingly filled bookcases of my childhood, augmented by my
mother's constant reading of novels (engaged in also by her two
sisters, when they were in residence for summers or holidays)
and by her comments that made me familiar with the names of
a great many authors before I could possibly have read them.
(My father had far less time to read but a greater interest in acquiring knowledge through reading, and he managed to fit in some
history and biography.) Whatever the primary causes of my
attraction to books, there are spots of time, still accessible to me,
that reflect stages in its growth. I remember being taught to read
by my mother on summer afternoons at my grandfather's farm,
while we were waiting for him to inspect the corn and cattle.
The fact that I can still vaguely recall the feel and look of the
books we read but can bring to mind nothing of the verbal content
may be a sign that I was particularly attentive to the physical
characteristics of books. Most children, of course, before they learn
to read, examine all the physical and visual features of their books,
not simply the pictures, because they rightly regard books as just
one more category of object; but unfortunately the process of
instruction in reading also seems to teach, by implication, the
irrelevance of a book's appearance. I do not know whether my
ability to recall something of the design of the first books I actually read suggests that I was an unwilling convert to an exclusive concentration on words. But there are indications that this
was so.

It seems revealing, for example, that the books I was given as
a child, most of which I still possess, generally look unread, though
I did read them. I have always had the urge to protect the books
I handled from physical harm; indeed, I rarely made marks in
any of my schoolbooks, even in college, preferring to keep notes
on separate sheets of paper. For some reason I remember being

especially attracted to a geography book I used in the fifth grade: not really a book of much visual appeal (being a typically drab textbook of the time, published by Ginn), but one that I liked the proportions of, proportions no doubt enhanced by the thought that the book, more literally than most, encompassed the world. Occasionally visiting lecturers performed at our high school on their book-promotion tours; and although I was not always enamored of their lectures, I did buy their books, just because I enjoyed handling them and placing them on my shelves. I regularly saved special issues of magazines (particularly when they included contributions by writers I had liked in my literature classes); and my most imaginative high-school acquisition – or so it seems to me in retrospect – was a magazine. During my junior year, in February 1950, Fleur Cowles began publishing her distinctive experiment, *Flair* (the magazine that became famous for the hole in the cover of each number); how I learned about it I no longer recall, but I know that I asked one of the local drugstores (which sold magazines) to order a copy for me each month. As a result, I have a complete file, in perfect condition, of the twelve numbers of this now sought-after journal (about which an elaborate book was recently published).

In my undergraduate years at Yale, I still did not consciously think of myself as a collector, but I did acquire the habit of browsing in used-book shops. Whitlock's basement ('The Crypt') became a favorite place of relaxation for me, and I think it must have been the first used-book store I was ever in. (My home town, Lebanon, Indiana, certainly had none; and despite its proximity to Indianapolis, I do not believe I had visited any such shop there.) All my literature courses at Yale affected my reading (and thinking) habits, but the one that was probably most influential was Norman Holmes Pearson's on twentieth-century American fiction. It began, imaginatively, with *The Education of Henry Adams*, included (innovatively for that time) Gertrude Stein and Nathanael West, and introduced me to several books that were revelations to me, such as *The Enormous Room* and *The Sound and the Fury*. In one of those moments that stay in the mind as pictures, I see myself sitting by the window of my ground-floor room in Timothy Dwight College entranced by *The Sound and the Fury*, which I was reading in the Modern Library edition (I can still visualize its dust jacket). Pearson impressed me not only by his lectures but also by the fact that he was a collector and a famous acquisitor for the Yale Collection of American Literature. Another of my Yale teachers for whom reading, scholarship, and collecting went hand in hand was Richard Little Purdy, whose collection I glimpsed several times as a result of his practice of asking students to visit his Berkeley College rooms to pick up their papers.

It was during graduate school at Northwestern that book-hunting came to occupy a sizeable portion of my time. The bookshops of Chicago were merely minutes away, and visiting them developed into a Saturday routine. At first I was buying books that I thought belonged in a well-rounded collection of English and American literature, without paying much attention to the particular editions – since I had not yet focused on the connections between texts and physical books (nor was I to encounter the concepts of analytical bibliography in any of my courses). Some purchases were titles I had learned about in class and wanted to read more fully (such as those of Thomas Browne and Laurence Sterne), but many were the works of authors, like Yeats and Stevens, that I had discovered outside of class and that had become important to me. I did also browse in new-book stores and occasionally picked up first printings of new works by Faulkner and the Beats, among others; in these cases, though I was indeed interested in the writers, I believe my principal concern was to secure 'firsts.' My specialized and systematic collecting began in 1958, when I started working on my dissertation. I had decided to write a biographical and critical study of Floyd Dell, novelist and radical journalist, because his rich and voluminous papers had recently been catalogued by the Newberry Library, and I liked the idea of being the first scholar to go through them. Because Dell was a central figure in the 'Chicago Renaissance' in 1909–13 and then in Greenwich Village, his life had connections with many writers who were significant in the formative years of modernism; and although most of the books I needed to study Dell and his contemporaries were available in the Newberry and Northwestern libraries, I naturally – it seemed natural to me – started buying them on my rounds of the bookstores. Thus my collecting acquired, for the first time, a sharp focus.

Even the unfocused years of book-hunting were an important part of my education, for they gave me some sense of a great many authors and titles I had not otherwise met with and – equally important, though I doubt that I knew so at the time – they acquainted me with the book designs characteristic of different times, places, and publishers. My subsequent purposive searching brought to light not only the books I was seeking but also related ones I did not know about, demonstrating to me the serendipity of research (or, more accurately, the fact that seemingly accidental discoveries come to those who are mentally prepared to find them). I put together runs of books by many writers whose lives intersected Dell's: Sherwood Anderson, Arthur Davison Ficke, George Cram Cook (founder of the Provincetown Players), Susan Glaspell, Eugene O'Neill, Edna St. Vincent Millay, and Randolph Bourne, to name a few, along with Dell's fellow-writers for the radical magazines, like Max Eastman. Although I drew from all parts of the Chicago area, my favorite source was Jerrold Nedwick's shop on Wabash Avenue, where my finds included many issues of *The Masses* and *The Liberator* and many books inscribed by prominent authors to the Chicago poet Eunice Tietjens. I felt so strongly about the role Nedwick played in my scholarly training that, after his death in 1967, I wrote a short memoir of him for *AB Bookman's Weekly* in which I called him 'an ideal bookseller for a book-collecting graduate student to encounter.' 'It is reassuring to a graduate student,' I went on, 'working day after day with relatively obscure figures (at least to him), to discover a person to whom these figures are more than names, someone who has talked with them, possesses association copies of their books, and knows all the stories behind them.' Under such guidance, I asked, 'who could fail to see more clearly (by contrast with the classroom) what education really meant?'

If my emphasis in these years was on authors, I was also becoming aware of the value of collecting for publishing history. That Knopf reprinted Dell's first novel, *Moon-Calf* (1920), nine times in ten months, for example, was something I could affirm by assembling copies of all ten printings, which in addition gave me the evidence for determining whether the text or presentation had been altered in the process. At this time I also began noticing that certain publishers' names – in particular, Mitchell Kennerley (publisher of Millay and Ficke) and B. W. Huebsch (publisher of Anderson and Bourne) – appeared on a number of the most interesting volumes in my Dell-related collection. So I started examining bookstore shelves for more books published by them and saw how revealing they were for understanding the publishing milieu out of which the other books emerged. The idea of collecting the output of certain publishers, thus formed, was encouraged by finding, on the top floor of the Central Book Store on Clark Street, several shelves of books published by the Chicago firm of Stone & Kimball (and its successor, Herbert S. Stone). They were remarkably cheap, and I decided to take them all, despite the fact that they were not directly related to Dell (dating from the years just before he arrived in Chicago) and that I had no desire to read most of them. But the firm was one of the most innovative in America in the 1890s, both in the content and in the design of its books, and I could not resist the urge to keep together such a substantial sampling of its output. With this act, I was clearly embarked on the collecting of publishers of two generations.

By the time I joined the English department at the University of Wisconsin in the autumn of 1960, there was no question about my thinking of myself as a collector. But, although I certainly understood how collecting supports scholarship, I did not yet think of myself as a bibliographical scholar. I did know about Fredson Bowers's *Principles of Bibliographical Description*, and I had already tried my hand at describing a few of my books, but I had only the vaguest sense of what bibliography as a scholarly field entailed. What changed this was my systematic reading of bibliographical journals. I became one of the stable of contributors to *Abstracts of English Studies*, and among the journals not being adequately covered were the major bibliographical ones. So I undertook the task (and continued with it for many years) of preparing abstracts of all the articles in *Studies in Bibliography*, *The Library*, *The Book Collector*, and *Papers of the Bibliographical Society of America*. In lieu of formal training, I could have had no better education than the discipline of writing summaries of all these articles, which introduced me to the kinds of work being undertaken – and to the range in the quality of thinking represented. (Although the published abstracts could not be critical, I was certainly aware, from the careful reading required, of the strengths and weaknesses of the pieces.) The exercise was so valuable that I eventually read the entire back files of these and other related journals, making notes not only on the articles but on the books reviewed. This process, which I pursued with great pleasure and satisfaction, soon gave me the confidence to undertake my own bibliographical investigations, and by mid-1964 I had contributed to the four major journals; in the previous year I taught my first graduate seminar on analytical and descriptive bibliography, printing and publishing history, and scholarly editing. My sylla-bus for that course reflected my self-education by providing exten-sive lists of books and articles, intended to suggest the scope and history of the field and to encourage students to browse in the publications that would give them direct experience of its developing arguments and accomplishments.

There were two occurrences in 1965 that symbolize for me how all my bookish interests are symbiotic. One was the publication in *Studies in Bibliography* of my article on 'The Historiography of American Literary Publishing,' which not only surveyed the literature of that field but also explained how to reconstruct the list of books brought out by any given publisher, a process I had engaged in for many of the publishers I collected. By then this group amounted to some forty firms between 1890 and 1930, little Village ones like Frank Shay (who published the series of Provincetown Plays) and Egmont Arens and much larger ones like Boni & Liveright and Alfred A. Knopf, and representing not only New York but Boston, Chicago, and San Francisco as well. The article made evident to me in a concrete way that every-thing I bought on the subject of publishing (including the imprint collections and also the numerous anniversary histories of pub-lishing firms and the like) supported my scholarly writing but was no less a 'collection' for that.

The other 1965 event was my starting work on the Northwestern-Newberry Edition of Melville's complete writings. I had been invited to join this project, as one of its three co-editors, by Harrison Hayford, the Northwestern professor who had directed my dis-sertation. This work, like the article, brought together several strands of my life: Melville was one of the authors I most enjoyed reading (and was the subject of my first published article); my particular responsibility on the Edition was printing and publishing history and textual policy; and this research, which entailed the locating and examining of multiple copies of Melville's early editions, required a knowledge of the collecting and antiquarian-bookselling world. Not only did these activities draw on the read-ing, writing, and collecting I had already done; they also, in their specific focus, involved demonstrating once again how texts (and thus meanings) are affected by the physical objects that carry them.

During the 1960s and 1970s, research trips (on Melville and other subjects) nourished my collecting as well as my writing. After work in libraries, all over Britain and the United States, I

visited any bookshops that were at hand. Among the highlights
of my annual visits to the West Coast were the hours I spent in
the great San Francisco shop of Warren Howell, who took a lively
interest in my imprint-collecting and regularly searched the shelves
along with me for items published by Doxey, Robertson, and Elder
(often retrieving from his office a book that had belonged to his
father). When I was in New York, the place I always went first
(as did many others) was the Seven Gables Bookshop; each
occasion was a treat, increased by a meal afterward with John
Kohn or Mike Papantonio, from whom I learned much. Not all
bookshops were so memorable, of course, but most of them yielded
something for me: year after year, as the thousands of bookshop-
visits mounted up, so did the thousands of books in my collection. By the late 1970s, I possessed some 15,000 volumes, about
two-thirds of them in my publisher-collections and one-third in
my books-about-books category (histories of all aspects of
bookmaking and collecting, descriptive bibliographies, landmarks
of textual criticism, and author-collections of the major writers
on analytical and descriptive bibliography and scholarly editing).
The books about books, I should emphasize, I do not regard as
simply for 'reference' but think of them in the same terms as all
my other collections – meaning that I pay attention to editions,
printings, jackets, and so on, regarding the physical features as
part of the information being conveyed. Only a portion of the
books about books, plus a large group of books on American
literature, would fit into my Langdon Street apartment in Madison;
all the others were in the Indiana house, enhancing by many
times the original assemblage that had so much affected me.

In 1978, Gordon N. Ray, president of the John Simon
Guggenheim Memorial Foundation, invited me to become its vice-
president. I was pleased to move to New York, which I was
thoroughly acquainted with from my many happy book-excursions
there over the previous quarter-century; but the move illustrates
in still other ways the influence that book-related associations
have had on my life. I first became acquainted with Gordon Ray
in 1969, when I received a Guggenheim Fellowship (which resulted
in my two-volume expansion of that 1965 'Historiography' article),
although I had known of him since my graduate-school days,
for he was one of the illustrious book-collectors of the century
and also a major literary scholar, having written the standard
biography of Thackeray. That he was also a great reader was

evident from his conversation; and the combination he represented – of reader, scholar, and collector, all obviously affecting
each other – naturally made him a figure of considerable interest
to me. I saw him when I visited New York after that, sometimes
in the Century Association or one of his favorite restaurants, and
sometimes at the Grolier Club, the bibliophilic society on 60th
Street that I became a member of in 1969. This acquaintance, tied
up with books in many ways, led to my being asked to join the
Foundation and to my feeling that it was an appropriate place
for a book-loving scholar to be.

I found an apartment – near the steps leading down from
Beekman Place to the East River – that would hold about 7500
volumes and still leave wall space for pictures; the rest of the
books remained in Indiana. From then on my life has continued
as it did before – reading and collecting books (adding another
5000 so far), writing about books and bibliography, editing (as
textual adviser to the Library of America), and teaching students
the connections among all these activities (in two courses for the
Columbia English department that have caused the old Wisconsin syllabus to grow into two sizeable publications). What has
changed is that I now have another connection to books – helping, through the Foundation, to provide people with the opportunity for writing more books. (The presence in the Foundation's
offices of an extensive library of books by Guggenheim Fellows,
plus the location of those offices only three blocks from both the
Morgan Library and the New York Public Library, maintains a
tradition important to me: for twenty-seven years – in New Haven,
in Evanston, where my address was Library Place, and in Madison
– I lived no more than two blocks from major university libraries.)

By now, with all the recent discussion that psychologists and
cultural critics have accorded the phenomenon of collecting, it is
well understood that objects play a crucial role in helping individuals to create stability in their lives. For me, books are the
objects, more than any other, that have been a unifying force,
joining inner and outer worlds and remaining as present reminders
of past events. Every book calls up the memory of a bookshop,
or a restaurant, or a town, or a companion, and it is these
associations, along with all the other roles of books in my life,
that make books such potent influences on the way I view my
destiny (just as other objects may serve for other people as landmarks of their lives). I do not consider it sentimental in any

pejorative sense to value these linkings – to connect a particular
book with a hot and dusty Fourth Avenue store and the lunch
at Lüchow's that followed; or another book with Peggy Christian's
La Cienega shop and dinner with her afterward, as always, at
St. Germain on Melrose Boulevard; or another with Dick Barnes's
wonderful Wells Street place and dinner with Harry and Jo
Hayford in Evanston, or Rick Johnson at The Bakery (owned by
a book collector); or another with an annual visit to Acres of
Books (the Cincinnati version) and its neighbor La Maisonette;
or another with Rota's Savile Row shop and lunch with John
Carter at the Westbury; or another with Larry McMurtry's (when
he was in Washington) and dinner with Bill and Nina Matheson
at Jean Louis; or another with Charles Traylen's by the castle in
Guildford and dinner with Jim Nelson; or another with Franklin
Gilliam's (in the Charlottesville years) and dinner with Fredson
Bowers and Nancy Hale, or Dave and Doris Vander Meulen; or
another with Harding's of Wells, Maine, and dinner in
Kennebunkport with my friend. (Our August drives to Northeast Harbor – on Mount Desert Island, Maine – include as many
bookshops and associated restaurants as we can manage. She
collects American publishers' bindings and has one of the outstanding collections of Margaret Armstrong's designs; because her
bindings and my publishers can turn up in any section of a shop,
we always have to inspect every shelf of every store.) There are
many cities in England that I probably would not have seen if
libraries or bookshops had not taken me to them, and many New
England villages I might have missed if they had not been the
locations of book-fairs or book-barns. The experience of each of
these places takes on a life of its own once I am there, and those
experiences are ultimately more important to me than the books.
But they might not have occurred without the books, and books
form the thread that ties them all together.

  Gordon Ray gave a talk in 1972 called 'Books as a Way of Life'
– a title I used for a posthumous collection of his essays, since
his own life perfectly exemplified the full meaning of that phrase.
In the speech, Ray was primarily concerned with the undogmatic
attitude of mind that often characterizes well-read people, who
have been exposed to a wide variety of ideas found in verbal
works. This receptive state of mind, he said, 'infuriates the fierce
partisan' by absorbing the attributes of what De Quincey called
the literature of power, which is – in Ray's marvelously incisive

phrasing – 'above politics, having understanding as its aim rather than victory.' And he added that the works embodying this attitude are 'a potentially unifying force in a divided world.' Ray's harmonious vision was the result, I am confident, not only of his encyclopedic reading but also of his intensive collecting, for he regarded the two as inseparable, and the two indeed work in partnership to produce the Miltonic calm of mind that he both described and experienced. In this context I always think of Nabokov's eloquent account of his feeling a 'sense of oneness with sun and stone' as he stood in a field among 'rare butterflies' – another instance (since Nabokov was a serious and accomplished butterfly-collector) of the way in which the knowledge and sense of control that derives from collecting is projected outward as one gazes beyond one's assembled objects.

My books, like Nabokov's butterflies, give me a setting from which I can venture with confidence and comprehension. And their ordered combinations and arrangements, like his of butterflies, create patterns for other people to encounter, just as I must assimilate what other people have constructed: I consider my collections of books no less a contribution to scholarship than the many words I have published. But such a contribution grows out of, and is likely to be proportionate to, personal equanimity and insight. As I look around me at the books I have lived with, understanding their contents, their place in intellectual history and in manufacturing history, their relationships to each other and to me, I know that I have mastered a small portion of the physical world and have given myself a framework for exploring other parts of it.

Part Two
Books of Our Own

5

Hooked . . .
NINA KING

As editor of the *Washington Post's Book World*, I recently asked
ten well-known authors to write about books that had changed
their lives. Their choices were sometimes odd, always interesting: Susan Sontag on travel writer Richard Halliburton's *Book of
Marvels*, Frank McCourt on Thomas Merton's *Seven Storey Mountain*, Kitty Kelley on *Huckleberry Finn*. They set me to looking for
comparable epiphanies in my own bookish life – in vain. I was
forced to an embarrassing conclusion: The book that changed
my life was *The Bobbsey Twins in the Country*.

Or perhaps it was *The Bobbsey Twins at the Seashore* or one of
the dozens of other titles in the series. In any event, it was the
first book I read all by myself. Not an auspicious choice for a
future book reviewer, this early twentieth century series was
hopelessly pallid, white-bread bland, casually racist. But the point
is not perspicacity but precocity: I was barely four and I had
taught myself to read.

So family legend has it. I have no memory of this feat of
autodidacticism, though I do retain an image of a small, presumably pre-school me sitting on the floor by a book shelf in my
grandmother's living room, reading one of the fifty or so
trademarked adventures attributed to one Laura Lee Hope and
starring 'dimpled' Flossie and Freddie (age four) and 'handsome'
Nan and Bert (age eight).

By the time I started school, I had left the Bobbseys behind
and moved on to Nancy Drew mysteries. I was certainly ahead
of the school primers featuring the monosyllabic exploits of Dick
and Jane and Spot. But I read them too – and repeatedly.

Thus a pattern was set early on: I would read anything in preference to nothing, and I would read in preference to doing almost
anything else.

I have no idea how I taught myself to read. But my learning surely had something to do with the many hours I had been read to by my mother and grandmother – from *The Wind in the Willows*, *Alice in Wonderland*, *Rabbit Hill*, *The Just So Stories* and all thirteen titles in the original 'Oz' series. Those hours – which did not cease when I started reading myself – were immensely pleasurable. They also bestowed an adult imprimatur on imaginative literature that, decades later, made the prospect of 'reading for a living' as the editor of a book review section seem respectable as well as entertaining.

But the kind of reader I have become is not really respectable. Yes, I passionately love certain books: those mentioned in the preceding paragraph, as well as the collected poems of Yeats and Larkin; *Emma* and *Pride and Prejudice*; The 'Lucia' novels of E.F. Benson; Kipling's *Kim*; anything by Angela Thirkell or Rex Stout, and almost anything by Graham Greene or Charles Dickens. I can read these books again and again. Nevertheless, I am less a bibliophile than I am a reading junkie, someone for whom the very act of reading has become an addiction, the printed word a drug.

My early experiments with the drug were rapturous, transcendent, at once escape and discovery. 'Each book was a world unto itself, and in it I took refuge,' writes Alberto Manguel of his childhood reading in his charming *History of Reading*. At eight or ten or thirteen or fifteen, I was, like Manguel, capable of total absorption in a book; no reading experiences since have ever been so sweet.

My youthful reading was extensive and eclectic. In a house full of books I was allowed free range, with some curious results. The triumphs of Cherry Ames, Student Nurse, alternated in my favor with the courtroom antics of Perry Mason; the death-defying exploits of the Prisoner of Zenda with those of Mary Poppins.

The only book I can recall being forbidden is *Gone With the Wind*. 'Wait until you're twelve,' said my mother. I didn't.

The first poem I learned by heart (and the only one I can reliably recite today) was John McCrae's 'In Flanders Fields,' a lament for the dead of World War I which ends with this mysterious peroration (what *could* it have meant to me?):

> Take up our quarrel with the foe:
> To you from failing hands we throw
> The torch; be yours to hold it high.

If ye break faith with us who die
We shall not sleep though poppies grow
In Flanders fields.

I first encountered the poem in a battered 1942 anthology called
A Treasury of the Familiar, a magpie collection ranging from the biblical account of Creation to 'The Cremation of Sam McGee.' The
compiler was one Ralph L. Woods. Most likely another reading junkie.

These days, though I can usually be *found* with my nose in a
book or other printed matter, rarely am I *lost* in it. More often I
am nodding off – succumbing yet again to drowsiness, the most
common side-effect of reading among aging addicts. '*La chair est
triste, hélas, et j'ai lu tous les livres*' (Flesh is sad, alas, and I've
read all the books), complained the poet Mallarmé. How did he
manage to stay awake that long?

It can be reassuring to compare notes with fellow addicts. But
like AA meetings such discussions usually degenerate into competitive horror stories:

'There I was on the Delta shuttle with nothing to read and no
airline magazine in the pocket...'

'Oh yeah, what about the safety instructions? At least you had
the safety instructions ... there was nothing *at all* to read on the
subway yesterday.'

The true addict cannot eat breakfast, fall asleep, ride a subway
or go to the bathroom without a supply of reading material, even
if it's printed on a shampoo bottle or a cereal box.

Manguel quotes Charles Lamb: 'When I am not walking, I am
reading. I cannot sit and think. Books think for me.' Perhaps the
darkest side-effect of addiction is this jittery inability to just sit
and think.

The brightest benefit is the escape that reading can offer from
a darkness within. It's a matter of finding the right drug. At a
time of marital crisis many years ago, I was quite unable to continue reading the biography of Queen Victoria I was halfway
through. Too real, I guess. Even that most buttoned-up of mon-
archs had emotions to which I, in my over-sensitized state,
resonated.

But Glinda the Good and Princess Ozma were made of different stuff. For six weeks, the only books I could read, the only
ones that could distract me from my banal woes, were set in the
Land of Oz.

6

Mountains and Caverns
ALAN SILLITOE

'Are the duties of the historians of hearts and souls inferior to those of the historians of external facts? Can we believe that Dante has less to say than Machiavelli? Is the lower part of civilisation, because it is deeper and more gloomy, less important than the upper? Do we know the mountain thoroughly if we do not know the caverns?'

On second thought perhaps I skipped that passage in *Les Misérables* when I first read it as a child, rather than face the ignominy of not understanding it. More to my taste would have been: 'Ships and barricades are the only two battlefields from which escape is impossible.' And so is life itself. But I read the book again and again in the next ten years, till most of it was fixed firmly in.

There was a public library less than a quarter of a mile from where we lived. The first time I went I was quietly pleased to note so many books that I could borrow three at a time for four-teen days. I stood just inside the barrier, and for a moment or two, till I became embarrassed at standing still too long in that exposed position, didn't quite know which of the racks and stacks to look in first.

Classified as a child, I could only get at baby stuff, William books, works by Conan Doyle, Rider Haggard, John Buchan. I gluttonously read my way from Montezuma's Daughter to the flat on Baker Street (both equally remote), and then asked the librarian if I could move into the grown-ups' section.

But when he said yes, I went back to reading Victor Hugo, because *Les Misérables* and *The Man Who Laughed* and *The Hunch-back of Notre Dame* and *The Toilers of the Sea* were closer to me than those aforementioned sub-classics of the English post-1870 Education Act literature. And rather than persist with Dickens, who for some reason I couldn't get into, I read books of travel (such as *France On Ten Pounds*) and books of instruction on how to write articles and stories, as well as histories, geography books, dictionaries – anything – apart from Hugo, with Dumas occasionally thrown in. A teacher at school, whose name was Charles Rowe (we called him Percy), saw my interest in geography and politics and lent me G. D. H. Cole's *Social History of Post War Europe*, a book beyond me at the time, though I appreciated his gesture.

I think *books* influenced me more than any title. I was entranced by the volume as an object, stiff covers between which were several hundred pages of magical symbols called *print*. I could flip them and cause a breeze against my cheek, thus demonstrating certain principles of physics. I could make a stack and see them from a few feet away as a pyramid of print, a Pennine of pages. They appeared to me as stepping stones to some state that I didn't yet know about.

Books were plentiful. They were cheap. In Frank Wore's secondhand shop downtown was a cellar with a vast table laden with threepenny volumes, and once the war started and there was more money I could afford at least one or two a week. In that cellar, where a coal fire burned on Saturday afternoons, and the smell of damp books and soot was so intense that I can still remember it clearly, no literary classic was beyond my reach. Yet I still preferred textbooks, crumbling lexicons, out-of-date one-volume encyclopaedias, old sixpenny cycling maps, Baedeker guidebooks – anything but fiction. I bought an immense leatherbound copy of the Book of Job in French, and read a few pages of that.

I hoarded books, and they caused a certain amount of resentment when I brought them into the house, especially from my father who thought I should spend my cash on something more worth while, such as food or shoes.

But with books I could cut myself off from everybody. I had a refuge – which my parents, brothers and sisters chose not to share or take advantage of. If they wanted to escape they were stuck to the mains wireless. I had only to walk away with a book in my hand.

Books took up space. They were intimidating. If you couldn't read, they were no good to you, so you wanted to kick them aside or sweep them off the table. When you did read, you went on reading, and the more you were absorbed, the quicker you got at the core of the books. The more you read, the more you wanted to read. Reading was mixed with the cinema, *Comic Cuts*, and the *Radio Times*.

I once saw a pyramid of hundreds of dictionaries outside the school stokehole waiting to be incinerated. With a friend I climbed over the high wall during one summer holiday when the place was deserted but for the caretaker, and saw this heap of redundant books. We couldn't understand why they had not been given out free, for all of us to take home. Admitted, most were in bad condition, but there was much use in them still. Along the wall, where they were waiting to be burned, it said in neatly painted white letters: Cleanliness is Next to Godliness – as if the world would be cleaner when fire had polished off these valuable books of words. We descended from our perch and thieved as many good copies as we could carry away.

The Second World War came and went, and I still read only textbooks, and books about the war itself. It is almost true to say that I read nothing that was adult till I was twenty. My teens were passed on other matters. After work in the factory I studied navigation, mathematics and meteorology, as an air cadet. Then there was the usual adolescent roistering to pass any spare time that remained.

In Malaya with the RAF, I was stuck for long hours to a radioset, so there was time to read. I'd brought in my kitbag from England a copy of the Old Testament. I met others who also read. A corporal threw me a copy of *The Ragged Trousered Philanthropists* after a long conversation about politics.

I picked up a volume which contained *Sevastopol* and *The Kreutzer Sonata* by Tolstoy in the camp library, and on the troopship I read *A Room With a View* by E. M. Forster, and *The Mutiny on the Elsinore* by Jack London. The fact that I remember the names of these books shows not only that they were 'memorable' in their content, but that it was rare for me to read a book at all.

At best it was random reading, and I couldn't much tell the difference between those books and *The Further Adventures of Jack the Ripper* – though the harder the book was (that is to say, the slower I was forced to read) the more I was aware that I was getting something out of it. Certainly, those early books were unforgettable in the density they seemed to possess.

When I got back to England at twenty, and had to go into hospital with tuberculosis, the real reading started. You name it,

I read it – in the following few years. One book I latched on to in hospital was *The Forest Giant* by Adrien le Corbeau, translated by T. E. Lawrence, and published by Jonathan Cape in the twenties. It was a slim book with rather nice woodcuts, a simple story of the birth and death of a tree by a river bank on the edge of a forest. It began as a minute seed falling from a mature parent and being washed down the river. Eventually it lodged on the bank and put out roots, and grew into an enormous 'forest giant' when the course of the river shifted. The book describes its life until, as a dying tree it falls into the dust and bracken.

The book was speckled with 'meaningful' sentences, such as (if I remember correctly: I wrote many down at the time but have lost the notebook): 'An incurable illness is a premature old age, and premature old age is an incurable illness.' Being, as far as I knew, incurably ill at the time, the sentence seemed profound and real. Maybe such a quotation is a bad example, however, and appears rather banal now, but that sort of writing was new to me, and somehow satisfying. It was like going back to a well of pure water I'd inadvertently strayed from.

I've looked for *The Forest Giant* in bookshops, libraries, and houses, but haven't found it. I'd be interested to read it again so as to see what attracted me to it, because it might indicate what my fluid half-formed biological mind was like at that time.

It is no use compiling a list of books I enjoyed. There are too many – and they wouldn't necessarily be the ones that influenced me. Those I liked obviously took me on an escape route away from one reality, but into another that seemed to enlarge my spirit because it allowed me to get a proper grip on my dreams. So I can mention *Nostromo*, *The Charterhouse of Parma*, *Moby-Dick*, *Tom Jones*, *Wuthering Heights*, *Tess of the D'Urbervilles*.

Those books that influenced me are the fundamental texts that hit me, sank so deeply I hardly felt their hidden purpose at the time. Or, what was also true, they stayed with me – or comforted me – at a time of crisis. It's not often possible to say which books these were, because what I read in them only takes effect many years after the crisis, rising up suddenly out of memory when I am not thinking about them, or when another hard knock is imminent.

While *Les Misérables* took me through the prolonged crisis of childhood, *The Forest Giant* helped me to manage the shock of my first illness when I thought I was going to die at twenty: I didn't care to go on living in a state of premature decrepitude. I recovered, as one might know, though it took nearly ten years, and I did it simply by ignoring the fact that I was ill – which is another kind of story.

In both cases I turned to a book and not to people, which must have some significance. The gift of literacy, and the universal accessibility of books, made a priest unnecessary. A self-educated sceptic is fairly independent in that respect.

Since I saw the devastating and healing importance of books it's not so strange that I decided to write one of my own. I looked for those that lent me their eyes, and allowed me to see things in the particular direction my mind and myself had always wanted to take – books that not only showed mé how to write, but which inspired me to write in a clear and comprehensible manner.

I won't go too much into that, because this is about reading, not writing – though I've never known how to keep the two separate. Writing fed on reading at first, till I could more or less see the mechanics of it. Then the writing fed on imagination and, last of all, on life itself – a meandering that finally brought the head back to the tail. But it was a long training of ten years, from the age of twenty to nearly thirty – though I don't suppose this is so long when, as Robert Graves states in *The White Goddess*, a Druid-poet went through a twenty-one year apprenticeship.

During the middle part of that decade I came across *Sand*, a forty-page work by Israel Joshua Singer – the best of many gems in a fat and priceless paperback-anthology of Yiddish stories. It is a simple tale of poor but religious people. They are also rough, primitive and quarrelsome: 'After all, a human being is a human being and does human things,' as one of the characters in it is forced to say.

We are taken through all the seasons of an isolated bone-poor settlement on the banks of the Vistula called Podgurna, and I shall always remember the description of the Russian artillery at the nearby fortress firing at the jammed ice-floes in spring, breaking them up so as to save villages from inundation – for which the inhabitants of Podgurna are touchingly grateful.

Reb Jonah, 'the elected rabbi and teacher and beadle and guide of Podgurna' had been taken off as a young man for twenty-five years' servitude in the Tsar's army, and in spite of all the indignities did not give up his religious beliefs. He fought bravely at Sevastopol and gained three medals. He was discharged in Siberia,

and spent some years officiating at a village synagogue there. As
an old man and a widower he comes back with his daughter
Mashka to Podgurna, where he was born – in the Jewish Pale of
Settlement.

When the people of the neighbouring and more important village
of Grobitze make harsh conditions for Podgurna about coming
to worship in its synagogue and using the burial ground, the
Podgurna people prevail on Reb Jonah to become their rabbi, so
that they can then be independent of the richer and snootier village.

This he does, though in a rather makeshift, inefficient fashion
regarding the tighter points of doctrine. He also runs the *cheder*
(school) to teach the children Hebrew, and marches them into
and out of his classroom like the old soldier he is.

Aaron, the travelling ritual slaughterer, recently widowed, comes
by from Grobitze, and is put up at Reb Jonah's house. He is well-
versed in the order of feast-days and ritual, so Reb Jonah is glad
to have him nearby to refresh his own hazy mind. Mashka, the
daughter, serves Aaron with his food, and he gets into her bed
one night, so that trouble really erupts when the women discover she is pregnant.

They don't find out till after she's given birth, in fact, and they
panic at the disgrace, horrified at what the self-righteous inhabitants of Grobitze will say. They flow into the humble synagogue
of Podgurna during a service conducted by Mashka's as yet un-
knowing pious grandfather. But Pesach Plotnik, the community
strongman, brings his meaty fist down on the pulpit and roars:
'Women and children, out of here! All of you, you bastards!'

Later he leads a foray against the neighbouring Grobitze, to
forcibly bring Aaron back, who is made to marry Reb Jonah's
daughter. At the wedding-feast you know that the young couple
are going to be as happy as any married pair will be after a few
years together. All has ended well, but it needed a whole community to put things right.

The story is much more than this bare outline, for it gets more
of life in it than most novels contain. It is the jewel of Israel
Joshua Singer's art – and I afterwards read all his novels and
stories, as well as those of his brother Isaac Bashevis Singer.
Together they have erected a permanent monument to a great
but (I'm grieved to say) vanished culture.

Strange as it may seem – though it never did to me – I felt a
strong connection between the people in these Yiddish stories

and those among whom I'd grown up in Nottingham. Though the novels I wrote during my stay in France and Majorca bore little relation to everyday life as I had lived it, my short stories did. They were set in Nottingham and concerned people I had known, or characters out of my imagination mixed in with the same realistic background.

I feel that if I had not read *Sand* I should not have written *The Loneliness of the Long Distance Runner* four years later, or *The Ragman's Daughter*, or *Mimic*. My stories would not have taken the *form* they did. *Sand* shows that much can happen between A and Z, that a tale is all the better – and richer – for being told in an unhurried, meandering and human way. Not sentimental, but moving and respectful of life. A man should live, if only to satisfy his curiosity.

Sand, a tale I picked at random, led me back and forth through the Yiddish anthology, to read *Kola Street*, *Repentance*, *White Chalah*, *Competitors* – and all the rest – and from them I saw that the historians of hearts and souls were not indeed inferior to those recorders of external facts. The two conditions met in these tales, and though I already knew that such was possible I was happy to find these fine examples of it.

A good time for reading a rich and stylish story is while on a train travelling alone. With strangers round about, and unfamiliar scenery passing the window (at which you glance now and again) the endearing and convoluted life coming out of the pages possesses its own peculiar and imprinting effects. An author has you firmly in his grip when his tale puts the rhythmically beating train wheel, out of your mind. A good book, an absorbing story, stops time, gives further distance to eyes that look inwards. And the greater distance in, the greater distance out.

I felt I had met many of those people from *Sand* before, both in literature and life. Literature belongs to the world, not to one country, and the story was like a country I had once lived in. I don't know why. The people are poor. They are vivid. They feel much. What's more, the author who wrote about their folly and suffering loved them.

People do not live in classes and masses, nations or groups. They are all of them individuals. When I see a long stretch of sand along a sea shore or river bank I know that not one grain is the same as any other, even though there are more than anybody can count.

I place *Sand* with a few other great short stories, and make the following list to show what I mean:

> *Sand* by Israel Joshua Singer.
> *A Gentleman from San Francisco* by Ivan Bunin.
> *The Heart of Darkness* by Joseph Conrad.
> *Lenz* by Georg Buechner.
> *Las Encantadas* by Herman Melville.
> *The Steppe* by Anton Chekhov.
> *The Sport of Destiny* by Schiller.

If I had them in one volume I would place it beside *Les Misérables* and the Old Testament, and row them to my desert island.

I'll also mention *The Anatomy of Melancholy*, by Robert Burton, a seventeenth-century priest endlessly expatiating on sin, concupiscence, plague, illness, ghosts, servitude, hypochondria, passion, love, madness, melancholy, medicine, superstition, despair, lycanthropy and jealousy – drawing in hundreds of obscure authors and classical quotations, and linking them in the richest of English commentaries – witty, profound, often misanthropic, but always creating a treasure-house of rare words, original compounds, and far-out anecdotes. It is the sort of packed marvellous idiosyncratic prose that can quench anyone's thirst in the desert of life.

So I stake my heart on that book as well, throw it in the boat to that hypothetical desert island even if it sinks it.

Such books make me, at certain times, happy to be alive, and glad to be a writer. I feel a sense of gratitude when I read those books again that helped me to know for sure who I was and what I wanted to do, books that were opening a door which I knew to exist, but did not have the key to till then, and which led me to the mysteries of the mountains and caverns.

7

Obsessed by Thomas Mann
JEFFREY MEYERS

I first read Mann's *Death in Venice and Seven Other Stories* in a Great Books course, during my freshman year at the University of Michigan, in 1955. As a rebellious teenager and would-be writer I was immediately fascinated by the intellectually rich and demanding fiction, full of symbols and allusions, which raised so many provocative questions. What makes an artist? Why must he oppose conventional society? How does he create? How does 'dangerous' music inspire him? Why must he suffer? How is disease related to art? As Mann, expounding one of his great themes, observed of two 'healthy' writers in 'Goethe and Tolstoy': 'Disease has two faces and a double relation to man and his human dignity. On the one hand it is hostile: by overstressing the physical, by throwing man back upon his body, it has a dehumanizing effect. On the other hand, it is possible to think and feel about illness as a highly dignified human phenomenon.... The genius of disease is more human than the genius of health.' The ambiguity of disease, its degradation and 'dignity,' was the crucial element in Mann's work.

I was then sixteen and remained puzzled after reading the stories. I didn't fully understand why, in 'Tristan,' Spinell drove the tubercular Gabriele to a fatal hemorrhage; why Tonio Kröger was suspect, even arrested as a criminal, when he returned to his home town; why Siegmund and Sieglinde committed incest in 'The Blood of the Walsungs'; why Aschenbach wanted Tadzio to die in 'Death in Venice'; why the deep family feeling in 'Disorder and Early Sorrow' was so melancholy and destructive; why Cipolla pushed Mario to murder in 'Mario and the Magician'? And the political implications of that act were also unclear. Later on, when I taught the stories, I would try to answer these crucial questions.

The seductive, disturbing element – the manifestation of *fin-de-siècle* decadence – impelled me toward Mann's other works. I devoured *Buddenbrooks*, clarified by my reading of 'Tonio Kröger,' and *The Magic Mountain*, foreshadowed by 'Tristan.' I was enchanted by Toni Buddenbrook, unhappily married to Grünlich, and by Hanno, who, as a little boy, writes his own death date in the massive family Bible. I was transfixed by the love affair of Hans Castorp and Clavdia Chauchat (and delighted to discover that her name meant 'hot cat') and, when their ideological disputes became deadlocked, by the climactic duel between Settembrini and Naphta. I then pressed on to the dauntingly complex allegory of the rise and fall of Nazism, *Doctor Faustus*, the perverse *Black Swan* and the coruscating *Confessions of Felix Krull*, in which the hero fakes a hilarious epileptic fit in order to dodge the draft.

Intrigued by the autobiographical elements and the portrayal of German social history – which had been demonized by the Hitler years – I came to admire Mann's elegant style, high art, penetrating irony, subtle wit, depth of meaning and insight into European culture. Though intellectual and philosophical, his novels had riveting stories and vivid characters. I loved the encyclopedic quality of *The Magic Mountain* and *Doctor Faustus* – there was so much to learn from them – and though I read the *Joseph and His Brothers* tetralogy to the very end, I found the copious Egyptology a bit trying.

After reading (while still in college) all of Mann's fiction, I turned to his essays, especially the ones on the five titans who had the most profound influence on his work: Goethe, Schopenhauer, Wagner, Nietzsche (Wagner's sometime friend and implacable enemy) and Freud. Mann's appreciative essays opened for me the doors to German literature, philosophy, psychology and music. Guided by Mann I read Goethe's *The Sorrows of Young Werther*, *Wilhelm Meister* and *Elective Affinities*; fought my way through the major chapters of Schopenhauer's *The World as Will and Idea*, especially the one 'On Death . . . ,' which Thomas Buddenbrook reads just before he dies; and (eventually) all of Nietzsche and Freud. I also saw Wagner's *The Flying Dutchman*, *Meistersingers* and *Tristan and Isolde*, but (despite Mann's enthusiasm) could never face *The Ring* and *Parsifal*. Nietzsche's incisive comment in *The Case of Wagner* – 'The problems he brings upon the stage – nothing but the problems of hysteria – the convulsive nature of his passions, his over-excited sensibility, his taste for sharper and sharper spices, his instability . . . not least his choice of heroes and heroines viewed as psychological types (a gallery of invalids): all this taken together represents a pathological pattern that leaves no room for doubt. *Wagner est une névrose'* – threw light on Mann's use of music to incite catastrophe in 'Tristan' and 'The Blood of the Walsungs,' on the record-playing chapter in *The Magic Mountain* and the diabolical compositions of Adrian Leverkühn (whose life is based on Nietzsche's) in *Doctor Faustus*.

I did not know German when I first read Mann. But I was eager to know his first, untranslated story, *'Gefallen,'* about a young medical student's love affair with an actress, which ends when he discovers an elderly rival has been paying for her services. So I persuaded one of my college girlfriends, who had spent her junior year in Munich, to read the story to me, translating it into English as she went along. After studying German in graduate school, I read Mann's *Die Entstehung des Doktor Faustus* (1949), a revelation of how he transformed reality into art, and Erika Mann's moving account of the very end of his life, *Das Letzter Jahr* (1958), to prepare for my Ph.D. language exam.

Inspired by Erich Heller's lecture on Mann at UCLA, perhaps the most dazzling I have ever heard, I also began to read all the books about him in English. The best critical studies, I found, were Heller's *Thomas Mann: The Ironic German* (1958), Gunilla Bergsten's *Thomas Mann's 'Doktor Faustus'* (1963) and T. J. Reed's *Thomas Mann: The Uses of Tradition* (1974). I then turned to the revealing memoirs by his wife Katia (1974) and his children: Klaus (1939 and 1942), Erika (1956), Monika (1960) and Golo (1986) as well as Michael's quite technical articles on his father's use of music. I gobbled up John Thirlwall's *In Another Language* (1966), about Mann's translator Helen Lowe-Porter, and the excellent biographies, as they began to appear in English: Nigel Hamilton's *The Brothers Mann* in 1978, Richard Winston's unfinished and posthumously published book in 1981 and, in a recent rush, lives by Ronald Hayman in 1994, Donald Prater in 1995 and Anthony Heilbut in 1996. Hamilton contributed an essay about writing his dual life of Thomas and Heinrich in *The Craft of Literary Biography*, which I edited in 1985. My friend Ronald Hayman eagerly took up my suggestion to write the first complete life of Mann in English. I put him in touch with Thomas' daughter Elisabeth, in Halifax, Nova Scotia, and read his typescript. Unlike most writers, Ronald was more interested in criticism than praise and we both enjoyed arguing about the contentious points in his book. I was delighted when he generously thanked me in the acknowledgments.

My obsession with Mann complemented my book collecting mania. I now own more than one hundred books in English and German by and about Mann, many of them acquired in used bookstores at astonishingly low prices. These include some rare pamphlets: *The Thomas Mann Commemoration* (Bryn Mawr, 1956), Golo Mann's *Memories of My Father* (Bonn, 1965), Joseph Campbell on myth in Mann (Mill Valley, California, 1973), and centenary essays delivered at Princeton and at Bad Godesberg in 1975. I also have the handsomely produced Knopf edition, with color-stamped and incised front cover, of *A Man and His Dog* (1930); a leather-bound American first edition of *Doctor Faustus* (1948); the elegant, privately printed *Letters of Thomas Mann to Caroline Newton* (Princeton, 1971); and the string-bound, blue-covered pamphlet, *An Exchange of Letters* (1937), in which Mann, nobly responding to the revocation of his honorary doctorate by the Nazi-controlled University of Bonn, concluded: '*God help our darkened and desecrated country and teach it to make its peace with the world and with itself!*'

But the pleasures of reading and collecting were not enough. I also wanted to deepen my understanding of Mann by seeing and hearing performances and adaptations of his works. I bought the 1952 Caedmon record, with notes by Monika Mann, of Thomas reading in German (as he often did to family and friends) from 'Tonio Kröger' and *The Holy Sinner*. I felt close to him, while following the text, as his deep, old man's voice pronounced the explosive words, describing the cold season, in the opening sentences of the story: 'The winter sun, poor ghost of itself, hung milky and wan behind layers of cloud above the huddled roofs of the town. In the gabled streets it was wet and windy and there came in gusts a sort of soft hail, not ice, not snow [*nicht Eis, nicht Schnee*].'

I attended a rare performance of his closet drama about Savonarola, *Fiorenza*, in San Francisco in 1961, and inspected the centenary exhibition at the British Museum. I saw Benjamin Britten's opera (1973), based on 'Death in Venice,' with Peter Pears in the leading role, and another opera (1994) based on 'Mario and the Magician.' I sat through the terribly dull films of *Buddenbrooks* (in silent and sound [1959] versions and in a television series [1984]), *Royal Highness* (1955) and *Tonio Kröger* (1965) as well as Horst Buchholz in the lively and frenetic *Felix Krull* (1957) and Dirk Bogarde in Luchino Visconti's slow but gorgeous *Death in Venice* (1971), in which Tadzio is a cheeky flirt and Aschenbach a pathetic degenerate. I once stood behind Bogarde on a passport inspection line before crossing the Channel to France and was eager to question him about his interpretation of the role. But, after driving his Lamborghini onto the ferry, he disappeared into a private cabin – possibly to avoid importunate queries like mine. None of these films was as good as the von Sternberg-Dietrich masterpiece, *The Blue Angel* (1930), based on Heinrich's novel. In the course of my travels I also saw, in Basel, Arnold Böcklin's painting *The Sacred Grove* (1842), which inspired Castorp's dream vision in *The Magic Mountain*, and, in Weimar, Werner Tübke's painting *Death in Venice* (1973).

During my annual summer trips to Europe I explored most of the places Mann had lived in and written about. Lübeck, his birthplace, near the Baltic coast, is the most beautiful town in Germany. The narrow streets of the medieval walled city, the busy river and port, the Gothic churches and Market Square, the Millwall and double-towered Holsten Gate, were all familiar to me from Mann's descriptions in *Buddenbrooks* and 'Tonio Kröger.' Mann was born in the so-called 'Buddenbrooks' house, which had been built by his grandfather, with a Baroque façade, in 1758. Destroyed and rebuilt after World War II, with a commemorative plaque, it is now a branch of the Volksbank. In Travemünde, northeast of Lübeck, a windy resort with high sand dunes, the Buddenbrooks took their summer holidays and Toni enjoyed a brief idyll with Morten Schwarzkopf before being married off, for dynastic reasons, to her horrid husband.

I visited Palestrina, east of Rome, a charming town where the composer was born, and where Thomas and Heinrich shared modest lodgings in 1895 while the younger brother worked on *Buddenbrooks*. In Munich, I saw his grand house on Poschingerstrasse and took the extended walk through the English Gardens and out to the North Cemetery that inspired Aschenbach's ill-fated journey to Venice. In Bad Tölz, an Alpine village south of Munich, on the banks of the Isar, I saw the country villa that Mann bought soon after his marriage. In Venice, the scene of his early masterpiece, I landed by boat (as Aschenbach had done) in the Piazza San Marco and strolled around the Grand Hôtel des Bains on the Lido. I still have the photograph I took in 1956 of a black hearse-gondola, with silver-painted angels at bow and stern, and the shimmering reflection of a balconied building upside down in the water of a canal. It would (publishers take note) make a superb illustration for the jacket of a new edition of the story.

In Davos, Switzerland, setting of *The Magic Mountain*, I searched for and found the Berghotel Schatzalp, once a tuberculosis sanatorium, where Mann had visited the ailing Katia in 1912. I could still see the partitions that separated the balconies and provided minor obstacles to the sexual adventures of the patients, the room in which Dr. Behrens examined the inmates and the glass door that Clavdia slammed dramatically to call attention to herself as she entered the dining room. Though the hotel was temporarily closed between seasons, the young Swiss girl who was minding the place allowed me to spend one evocative night there. After dinner (like Castorp and the other *moribundi*) we stretched out on the chaise longues, wrapped ourselves in blankets and gazed dreamily at the glittering stars and snow-capped mountains lit by moonlight. Lonely in that vast establishment, the Swiss girl was eager to be seduced (once I unravelled her complex undergarments). I also owe that romantic episode to Thomas Mann.

While teaching at UCLA in 1963, twelve years after Mann had left California, I looked up his address in an old phone book and presented myself at the door of 1550 San Remo Drive in Pacific Palisades. Surprised and pleased that I had connected their house with the eminent author, the current owners – in friendly American fashion – invited me in for a tour of the house and garden, and view of the Pacific. When I asked for a glimpse of Mann's relics, they showed me a poster he had left behind of a black madonna in Czechoslovakia and a modest side table that still stood in the hallway. Inspired by photographs of Mann sitting in his California garden, wearing a white suit, white shoes and Panama hat, and hoping they would provide inspiration, I promptly acquired the ensemble. *Anch'io son scrittore!*

Finally, I made a pilgrimage to Kilchberg, outside Zurich and with a fine view of the lake, where Mann spent his last four years. I also visited Fluntern cemetery, where he is buried quite close to James Joyce. Like many other foreigners – Rilke, Stefan George, Musil, Hesse, Remarque, Nabokov, Silone, Irwin Shaw, Borges, Simenon and Graham Greene – Mann died in Switzerland, where, as Scott Fitzgerald observed, 'very few things begin, but many things end.'

Having exhausted all the Mann sites in Europe, I extended my explorations to the literary places that had inspired him. I visited Dürer's high-gabled, cross-timbered house in Nuremberg, which Mann described in *Doctor Faustus*; Goethe's house in Weimar, which Mann portrayed in *The Beloved Returns*; Wagner's fortress-like residence, Wahnfried, in Beyreuth, which Mann calls Einfried in 'Tristan,' as well as Nietzsche's summer retreat in Sils Maria, Switzerland, and Freud's apartment, which Mann also visited, on Berggasse in Vienna.

But my obsession also required contact with people who knew Mann. During my senior year at Michigan, when I told one of my teachers about my all-consuming interest, he suggested I see Hans Meisel, a professor of political science, who had been Mann's secretary in Princeton in the late 1930s. Impressed at first by my intense curiosity, Meisel patiently answered all my questions. But – puffing on a cigarette while holding it, European fashion, between his thumb and index finger – he eventually became weary of my all too frequent visits to his office. To get rid of me for a month or so, he would tell me to read some long and difficult books. But this only fueled my appetite and he was astonished when, my happy task completed, I appeared the following week with a great many more questions. His reading lists got longer and longer until, with my classes and job, I was unable to cope with them. Though Meisel finally got rid of me, he was inordinately tolerant.

While working at a beach club on Long Island after returning from my junior year in Europe, I met a minor poet, David Posner, the first creative writer I had ever known. He told me that when he was at prep school (I think it was Lawrenceville) near Princeton, some of the boys used to go to Mann's house. But after a few disturbing incidents, all visits were forbidden. I therefore knew, as early as 1958, that the homosexual longings described in 'Tonio Kröger' and 'Death in Venice,' in *The Magic Mountain* and *Doctor Faustus*, were actually based on Mann's personal feelings. This secret was not revealed in his biographies until the 1990s. Of Mann's six children, Erika, Klaus and Golo were homosexual.

During my first year in graduate school, at Harvard, I heard that Michael Mann, Thomas' youngest son, had given up his career as a professional violinist and, in his forties, was studying for a doctorate in German. I met him in Cambridge and again in Berkeley, where I subsequently transferred and where he became an assistant professor. (Einstein's son and Renoir's grandson were also on the faculty.) I was struck by the astonishing good looks of Michael, his Swiss wife Gret and his son Frido, the model for Leverkühn's angelic nephew Nepo, who dies in ghastly fashion from meningitis in *Doctor Faustus*. When I asked Michael about his father, he said 'I didn't really know him.' He had been brought up by his nursemaid and governess. By the time he was old enough to sit at the family table, his father had won the Nobel Prize and hardened into a remote and imperious figure who had very little time to spend with small children. Later on, I heard rumors that Michael, like Klaus, had committed suicide and this was sadly confirmed in Prater's biography.

In 1975, when I was editing *George Orwell: The Critical Heritage*, I corresponded with Golo Mann, then teaching history at Claremont College. He gave me permission to translate (with a German friend) and reprint his incisive review of *Nineteen Eighty-Four* that had appeared in the *Frankfurt Rundschau* in November 1949. Through Michael and Golo I secured an invitation to visit Mann's nonagenarian widow in their house in Kilchberg. I brought along, as a gift, an early review copy of the American edition of her memoirs and presented it to her. She offered me high tea and seemed pleased to have some news from America. But every so often – two or three times in the course of my brief visit – she would suddenly stop the conversation in English, stare at me and disconcertingly ask: *'Aber, wirklich, wer sind Sie?'* ('But, really, who are you?') I would lamely justify my presence, even my existence, and we would carry on our talk until she once again forgot who I was and why I was there. I have always thought Katia's – *'Aber, wirklich, wer sind Sie?'* – would make a fine title for an autobiography.

All the knowledge I had acquired about Mann's life, works and milieu were immensely stimulating. I had taught his stories and novels every year, and kept up with his *Letters*, *Diaries* and *Reflections on a Non-Political Man* as they appeared. But my obsession could not be satisfied until I had *done* something with Mann and made him my own. So I finally began to write about him. Between 1971 and 1986 I reviewed Mann's *Letters*, T. J. Reed's study, the Hesse-Mann correspondence, Katia's memoir, and the biographies of Hamilton and Winston.

I also began to publish critical essays and chapters about Mann in my books. 'Shakespeare and *Doctor Faustus*' (*Modern Fiction*

Studies, Winter 1973) argued that the seeds of Leverkühn's genius
and the tragic pattern of his allegorical life are foreshadowed in
his demonically inspired adaptation of *Love's Labour's Lost*. 'Caligari
and Cipolla: Mann's "Mario and the Magician"' (*Modern Fiction
Studies*, Summer 1986) showed how the vivid detail, innovative
technique and psychological power of the classic Expressionist
film, *The Cabinet of Dr. Caligari* (1919), influenced Mann's story.

The chapter on 'Dürer and *Doctor Faustus*' in *Painting and the
Novel* (1975) reproduced Dürer's engravings, *Melencolia* and *The
Martyrdom of St. John the Evangelist*, and described how they relate
Leverkühn to the frenzied world of the German Reformation.
Dürer's art visualizes the themes of artistic sterility, fiendish suf-
fering and apocalyptic destruction. (I also bought an engraving
of St. Simon, which Dürer made in 1523 and, 475 years later,
hangs in my study.)

The chapter on 'Death in Venice' in *Homosexuality and Literature, 1890–1930* (1977) concluded that in the doomed love of the
suspect pederast, Mann found the perfect pattern for the artist's
desperate struggle to recapture the ideal form of sensual beauty,
to unite passion with thought, grace with wisdom, the real with
the ideal.

I analyzed three of Mann's works in *Disease and the Novel, 1880–
1960* (1985). In *The Magic Mountain* Mann uses realistic clinical
details for satiric and tragic effect, portrays a medical institution
and relates this special world to the ideological crises that led to
the carnage of 1914. At the end of *Doctor Faustus* the musical,
military, pathological and political themes brilliantly merge as the
four stages of Leverkühn's syphilitic disease – migraines, infec-
tion, remission and collapse – tragically fuse with Germany's
predisposition to Reformation-inspired demonology, deliberate
choice of Nazism, decade of military conquest and disastrous
devastation. The disgusting clinical details of *The Black Swan* (1953),
a late minor work, express Mann's cathartic defense against old
age and poor health. They prove that Mann, who had recovered
from a lung cancer operation in 1946, could himself face the ugly
and terrifying reality of death.

I have been reading Mann for more than forty years, and my
admiration for and delight in his art remain intense. He inspired
me to learn German and led me to European fiction, music and
painting. He incited me to travel throughout the continent (and
even to Egypt) and to seek out people who knew him. He made

me want to teach literature in college. The research, pilgrimages and interviews, the pursuit of a real person who left a trail through life and history, made me a biographer.

   Mann is still very much in my thoughts. I have recently reviewed the *Letters of Heinrich and Thomas Mann* and written an essay on 'Family Memoirs of Thomas Mann.' I have also completed a screen adaptation of *The Magic Mountain*, using the Alpine setting and morbid atmosphere, and focusing on the love affair of Hans and Clavdia. As she tells Hans, the equally obsessed hero of the novel, 'You won't get away from me, little one': *'Tu ne m'échapperas, mon petit.'*

8

Encountering Philip Larkin
DALE SALWAK

When Robert Frost read one of D. H. Lawrence's poems he observed, 'it was such a poem that I wanted to go right to the man that wrote it and say something.' That was just the feeling I got when reading for the first time Philip Larkin's 'Church Going' – to this day one of my favorite of his poems, and of course one of the most-anthologized. I can't read his poems without wanting to say something to the author.

My very first encounter with the name 'Philip Larkin' occurred in 1967, when as a student at Purdue University, I had been assigned to read and report on Kingsley Amis's novel *Lucky Jim* in the context of the so-called 'Angry Young Men.' I noted the dedication page of that novel and asked my professor, 'Who is Philip Larkin?'

With enthusiasm he loaned me his copy of *Jill*, and that led to *A Girl in Winter*, then to *The Less Deceived* and *The Whitsun Weddings*, and much later to the other prose. Here was an alternative, a refreshing change from so much contemporary poetry that seemed at times too abstruse or too specialized or too private to be understood. Here was a poet who spoke directly and beautifully and often amusingly about subjects that – even as a youthful undergraduate – I recognized and cared about and thought about. I sensed what Larkin meant when he wrote, 'The essence of [the poet's] gifts is to create the familiar, and it is from the familiar that he draws his strength.'

Not that I always understood what I read. Eliot has written, 'A poem can communicate before it is fully understood,' and I think

This essay is excerpted from a longer version presented at the Philip Larkin Society, Hull, England, on 25 February 1997. Two different versions appeared, respectively, in *Biography*, XXI (1998), and *About Larkin*, #5 (1998).

that was my experience. I was nineteen at the time, had never been to England and knew little of English life and literature, and so no doubt I missed the full impact of all sorts of references in Larkin's poetry that came from his milieu. Sometimes I had to refer to the dictionary just to understand a line. Jenny Joseph has written in *Philip Larkin 1922–1985: A Tribute* of a similar experience when reading the 'enticingly referential' poetry of John Ashbery: 'Although an English person knows that the richness is there,' she says, 'I feel I'm getting it slightly out of focus, blurred when it is particularly exact.'

Moreover, what devices for unlocking poetry I had acquired came to me primarily by way of our study of the modernists – Yeats, Pound, most particularly Eliot, who wrote in 1921, 'The poet must become more comprehensive, more allusive, more indirect, in order to force, to dislocate if necessary, language into live meaning.' Because modern life is complex and difficult to grasp, as that argument runs, the poetry that interprets it must itself be complex and difficult to grasp.

But that attitude also helps to explain why many of us continued to read Larkin during our college years and carried him into our graduate study years. We could savor the richness without struggling with the obscurity. Derek Walcott put it beautifully when he wrote for *The New York Review of Books* (1 June 1989):

> No other poet I know of makes the reader an intimate listener as well as Larkin does. The poems are not confessional, they are shared with the reader, with the joke always turning on Larkin. . . . Larkin is a moral poet, an honest one, who hated grandeur and the posing that encourages experiment. This is not conservatism, it is, purely, devotion. And this is why poets will continue to cherish him beyond his current popularity – for that crisp dismissal of 'What's not good enough,' or what 'has nothing to say.'

Certainly the culmination of my own admiration for Philip occurred when I was able to meet him, first in 1982, and again shortly before he died, in 1985. In 1980, upon learning of my love for twentieth-century English literature, and of my particular admiration for Philip Larkin, Eddie Dawes – a professor of biochemistry at the University of Hull and fellow conjuror – asked if I would like to meet the man. Eddie said he knew him and that they worked together on the library committee. 'Although Philip is a shy man,' Eddie wrote, 'it should not be too difficult to set up a dinner party for you to meet him.'

It wasn't until two years later, when I was finally able to travel to England again, that I had that opportunity at the Dawes' home. The event was completely stage-managed by Eddie, who had suggested to Larkin that he come to the house for a brief private performance of magic. Larkin was wary and shied away from the thought that he would have to discuss his poems, but Eddie reassured him. He accepted and arrived promptly at 7 p.m. dressed in a black suit, white shirt and dark green knitted tie, and carrying a brown briefcase in which he had brought copies of some review articles I had previously requested. Having driven himself, he complained how he had almost lost his way. He sat down, had a gin-and-tonic, and then we enjoyed one of Amy Dawes' splendid dinners. Afterwards we moved upstairs to Eddie's magic room and performed a show for Philip, including the three-card trick, which he took part in himself. The next day he invited me to his office, where he left me alone for an hour with his archives, and I noted those items from English journals that I didn't have, which he promised to copy for me. When I told him that I had in mind an annotated bibliography on him much like the one I had done in 1978 on Kingsley Amis, Larkin looked up quickly from his desk and said, 'Sounds like a super-Bloomfield.' I left Hull the next day.

In July 1985, at lunch with Kingsley Amis, I learned of the seriousness of Philip's illness – something Eddie had alerted me to in an earlier letter. When I mentioned that I was going to Hull, Amis said, 'Surely you don't intend to see Philip.' I said I hoped to, but he shook his head, saying he wasn't well. (Much later I learned that neither Kingsley nor his first wife, Hilly, had ever seen Larkin's home in Hull.) My wife Patti and I traveled to Eddie's not expecting to see Philip, but that morning Eddie called Philip, who said, 'Yes, please come over.' We arrived at 10 a.m. and sat in his Newland Park home #105, in the sitting room for an hour. He apologized that Monica Jones couldn't come down but she wasn't well. He sat in his chair, I to his left, then Patti on the couch with Eddie. Philip seemed hard of hearing, but spoke with great interest. He thanked me again for the show three years before, said he had been so moved by it that when he returned home he had written about it in his journal. 'I should show you what I wrote,' he said, but the opportunity never developed. Next he asked how the Barbara Pym book was coming along, to which he had contributed an essay. And we talked about Kingsley Amis, about whom I was writing at the time, and I mentioned that I'd love to show Kingsley my magic, too.

As the hour drew to a close Eddie took out his camera and Philip sat between Patti and me on the couch with an arm around each of us. He drew Patti close to him and said to her – she was twenty-five at the time – 'You could be my granddaughter.' Patti took to him right away; afterwards I asked her impressions, and she said two words: sensitive and vulnerable. Like me, she was much moved by the gentleness of the man, and the melancholy.

Eddie's flashbulb did not work, and so we went outside and there took the picture that I later reproduced in an anthology I edited. Under my arm I carried a copy of *All What Jazz* with the inscription: 'From Philip Larkin in the shade to Dale and Patti in the sun (temporarily and permanently, respectively, we hope).' A day later he called Kingsley to say he'd like to hear his reaction to the magic show.

'We're all very excited about seeing your magic,' said Kingsley to me the next morning over the telephone. And so yet another dinner party was set up, followed by a show – this time at Kingsley's home, and all because Philip had followed up on my comment the previous day. I have since learned that Kingsley retold the story of how I had met and entertained Philip, always with humorous embellishments.

Andrew Motion tells us that 'as [Larkin] grew older he was more inclined to show each of his correspondents the face he knew would please them most.' Every one of the thirty-seven letters I received from him – some handwritten, many typed – bears the stamp of Philip in various ways, by turns warm, humorous, helpful, self-deprecating, generous, poignant, and always encouraging – someone with whom I wish I had spent more time, someone to whom I wish I had written more often. For he always answered my letters, and apologized when he delayed in doing so. Only later did I fully appreciate that Larkin's private correspondence was for him what someone has called a kind of consolation and healing. As he wrote in 'Aubade,' 'Postmen like doctors go from house to house.'

The earliest letter I received from him is dated 9 June 1981. Eddie Dawes had very kindly passed along to Philip one of my books, and he wrote to thank me and say, 'I see . . . that you have rather specialised in British authors of the Fifties, and hope it has not proved too distressing. I think you deserve a spell of Tennessee Williams.'

On 25 August 1982, he expressed 'a deep sense of gratitude' for the magic show that Eddie and I had presented, and said: 'I have gone round telling people about it. My publisher asked me if I knew the story of the juggler and the statue of the Virgin Mary, which apparently ended with a deep and disembodied voice saying, "Don't call us, we'll call you," but I expect you've heard that.'

In that same letter, 'Since our meeting I have duly become weighed down with my sixtieth year, which all seems very odd. "Now of my three score years and ten, Three score will not come again," I remarked to our archivist, who replied (well, almost) "And very soon I'll be bereft of the ten singles that are left" (he is almost exactly the same age). So you see, poetry is not a specialism round here.'

Upon hearing from Eddie of my marriage, he wrote on 21 December 1983, 'I hasten to offer my congratulations, if a bachelor's congratulations on such a matter are worth anything. At any rate, if you do come this way next summer, as you hint, I shall be delighted to see you both.'

About the appearance of *Required Writing*, he wrote in the same letter, 'I expect by now you will have heard of my collection of oddments. . . . The reviews it has had have been far too favourable; very soon someone will cut me down to size, and not before time.'

University of Hull affairs sometimes entered his letters, too, as on 5 January 1983: 'The University here has offered me the choice of having my arms or legs chopped off (professionally, I mean), and I am just composing my reply. It will probably fall to Eddie to hold me down.'

Or on 19 March 1984, 'We had a sit-in here last week, and Eddie (who is my Chairman) came from compeering [*sic*] a conjuring show to help me patrol the body-strewn floors. I wish he could have made them all disappear.'

When I asked if he would consider submitting an essay on Barbara Pym for a collection that I was editing (he did), he wrote: 'You mustn't think of me as a scholar – just a hack reviewer' and offered to contact on my behalf another possible contributor, A. N. Wilson. 'I met Andrew Wilson in Oxford recently,' he wrote in another letter. 'I tried to impress him with the worthiness of the project.'

On 26 April 1985, when I asked if I might interview him for a book I was writing on Kingsley Amis, he replied at length: 'I feel uncertain . . . how far I should be able to help either you or Mr. [Julian] Barnes [also thinking of writing one] in any practical way. I have never had much critical ability, and Kingsley strikes me as an above-average difficult case for comments of this kind. As for the personal side, well, without suggesting that Kingsley has any special skeletons in his cupboard I should be rather reluctant to do anything approaching gossip about him, if only because he might do the same about me one day. So you may find yourself in the position of trying to get blood out of a stone! However, as a magician, this should present no problems – to you!'

On 15 September 1985 – my last communication with him – I sent by overnight mail a letter asking Larkin if he would con- sider writing in support of my application for a fellowship to cover another trip to England, and he wrote by hand five days later, 'Your letter arrived this morning with full honours of bell- ringing and receipt-signing. $23.00! That's a lot of money. I only hope this more humble communication will take less than a week.' And regarding my application, 'Well, all right, but *caveat emptor* – I will act if you are prepared to risk it.'

In that same letter: 'I suppose I am getting better slowly, but the whole business has led to rather a crisis of confidence. To go through the ice of daily life means you can never forget how thin that ice is – you are always listening for the next cracking.'

That cracking would come sooner than any of us could guess. On 2 December, early in the morning, I was awakened by my wife's gentle touch on the shoulder, and opened my eyes. 'Dale, Philip Larkin has died.'

I can't imagine the distress that those close to him must have felt on that day, or the totality of the loss they must continue to feel thirteen years later. I know that I was filled with regret, but also gratitude that I had had a chance to meet the great one, and that my wife had as well.

The American consensus is that Philip Larkin was a very good poet who knew how to say serious things about serious subjects. We do not read him as simply the crusty provincial grinding away about old rundown Britannia, nor are we distracted by the many cynical voices that have made themselves heard since Philip died.

He speaks to our condition. 'One can only marvel,' wrote Bryan Aubrey, 'that from the pen of a man who so often was oppressed by the weight of living came poems of such unblinking honesty, such clear-cut, glistening beauty... and such subtle, controlled power – brief moments of perfection quarried from the chaos of a life.' In *The New Yorker* (17 July 1989), Clive James wrote that Larkin's voice 'made misery beautiful,' and I cannot improve on that judgment. James continued, the impact that Larkin said Bechet made on him 'was exactly the impact that Larkin made on readers coming to him for the first time':

> On me your voice falls as they say love should,
> Like an enormous yes.
> ('For Sydney Bechet')

Or as J. D. McClatchy wrote of him two months earlier in *The New York Times Book Review* (21 May 1989), 'when most of the flashier, more blustery contemporary literature has passed away, his poetry – ghostly, heartbreaking, exhilarating – will continue to haunt.'

Recently I had cause to reflect upon some of the reactions to the life of Larkin since his passing. While it is true that his reputation in America is slim, that he does not possess what Martin Amis has called in *Vanity Fair* (April 1986) the 'inescapable presence' that he has in England, his name has always been very much alive among serious readers of poetry ever since the publication in 1955 of *The Less Deceived*. That presence grew significantly in 1988 with the publication of *Collected Poems*, which finally made his poetic work accessible to a wider reading audience. The controversy that has swirled around Andrew Motion's biography and Anthony Thwaite's edition of the *Selected Letters* has also added breadth to Larkin's reputation.

'Poor Philip Larkin,' wrote the American reviewer Bryan Aubrey on the occasion of the publication of the *Selected Letters*. 'At the time of his death in 1985, he held an exalted position as one of the finest and most read poets in England since World War II. . . . Since then, however, Larkin's reputation has taken a nosedive. Part of this results from the inevitable reappraisal that every poet undergoes after death. For Larkin, however, it seems a case of his having done himself in, so to speak' (*Magill's Literary Annual 1994*). As his reputation grew and information about him became more accessible, those who knew Larkin primarily from his published writings were not prepared to see how often his private correspondence contained revelations of his complicated love life, his affinity for pornography, and his sometimes strident, right-wing, racist, xenophobic views. If there is a theme that runs through many of the critical responses in England at the time of the *Selected Letters'* publication, it is in effect, we thought Larkin one of the greatest English poets of our time. How he deceived us!

Aubrey goes on: 'Motion's biography did nothing to rehabilitate Larkin, and in England it set off another cavalry charge aimed not only at the man but also at his poetry.' That charge had its effects across the Atlantic: Originally, the volume of letters was to be published in America in January 1993, but the publishers postponed it for eleven months, fearful that its reception would adversely affect sales of Motion's biography, which was published that summer.

Martin Amis opened a pre-emptive defense of Larkin in *The New Yorker* (12 July 1993) by saying, 'The reaction against Larkin has been unprecedentedly violent, as well as unprecedentedly hypocritical, tendentious, and smug. Its energy does not – could not – derive from literature: it derives from ideology, or from the vaguer promptings of a new ethos.' And then he went on to rebut one-by-one each of the charges against Larkin: pornography, sexism, misogyny, racism, lack of progress in his life, his gloom. Nevertheless, as William Pritchard has noted in *The New York Times Book Review* (1 August 1993), advanced publicity directed attention to Larkin's bad attitudes, 'with the effect of alerting people who had no interest in reading his poems anyway to the scandal of the poet as unacceptable human being.' In more than one instance, I know of readers who turned to the biography without ever having read the poems – in search for anything even remotely scandalous.

Could Larkin really have been as bad as all that? Even if he was, does it matter? These are among the questions stated or implied by many of the American reviewers. While dismayed by some of the glimpses into Larkin's private side and surprised if not shocked by the fury of reactions in the British press, most reviewers tended to focus sympathetically on the subject's unhappiness and quickly came forward with reasons why both the *Letters* and the *Life* – with their revelations of unsuspected foibles,

weaknesses, inconsistencies, and faults – should not seriously diminish our admiration of Larkin's gifts. The poet's first duty is
to be true to himself; Larkin had a perfect right to express the
depressing aspects of that self, just as he expressed its humorous
or kind or sympathetic facets.

'Why,' Pritchard goes on, 'would one want to read all this when
the matchless poems are there, still fresh and glittering as creation
itself? Because, if we decide that these poems constitute a great
creative achievement, we want to know everything, even too much,
about the man who wrote them.' Yes, we want to know all we
can about the artist, but as Bernard Knox said recently at a meeting
of the Association of Literary Scholars and Critics, 'the facts of
the author's life should not be allowed to obtrude their presence
into judgment of the work, especially if, as so often happens,
perfection of the work is not matched by perfection of the life.'

Many commentators agree. Christopher Porterfield (*Time*, 6
September 1993) calls Larkin's coarseness, his penchant for pornography, and his racist remarks 'boisterous role-playing.' Joseph
Epstein (*Commentary*, April 1994) calls the biography 'oddly
prosecutorial,' but sees the letters as penned by 'a good-hearted
man who could write with exquisite tact to a woman . . . ; who
could soothe friends in their grief, stick by them in their suffering . . . , entertain them in their boredom, delight them with his
faithful attention. The occasional politically-incorrect opinions have
obscured the fact that there is scarcely a letter in the *Selected
Letters* that does not contain something charming, touching, funny,
or generous.' Epstein goes on to laud Larkin as 'a man unable to
lie about his experience and who, no matter how dark or even
pathetic that experience, finds reason to laugh about it.'

Diane Middlebrook in *The Hudson Review* (1994) comments on
Motion's views, noting that 'Every biographer is situated in some
mode of social relationship to the worthy under discussion. I think
Motion has chosen . . . the most productive relation to the problem of Larkin's character: that of son and heir to *mon semblable,
mon père.*' Nonetheless, Middlebrook admits that while 'Larkin's
public demeanor was polite, reserved, and funny' and 'people
loved being with him,' the 'crudities isolated from his private
communications are being held against him now, because of their
power to diminish the character-ideal Larkin had become for the
British public: an island of personality traits deduced from the
speaking voice in his poems.'

Or as Vereen Bell in *The Southern Review* (1994) puts it, Larkin, like Eliot, 'became in his poems the best possible version of himself.'

In very quick time, therefore, the controversy – provoked when the refinement of the poems came up against the coarseness of the life – died out, and while Tom Paulin may continue to write letters to the *TLS* raving on about 'the sewer beneath the national monument,' few in America are listening (see, for example, *TLS*, 6 November 1992). They are too busy rereading the poems and the novels, discovering the art anew, and most readers dismiss the attacks in the press as mere *argumentum ad hominem*.

Probably all of us who are avid readers of biography have a list of individuals from the past whose lifestyles are not particularly appealing to us. My own life would be less rich if I eliminated from my shelves the works by those musicians, artists, and writers whose lives or morals I didn't necessarily agree with. Should those revelations in any way deter us from wanting to read an artist's work? Should they affect our assessment of that work, other than open up perhaps wider possibilities of interpretation? For any writer there is bound to be more than one kind of personal or literary reputation, and the portrait that gets into the literary history books is not the only possible likeness. 'The words of a dead man/ Are modified in the guts of the living,' Auden has told us ('In Memory of W. B. Yeats'), and when public and private personalities enter the picture, their seeming disparity often makes it difficult to get to the creator's art. In his essay 'Samuel Johnson's "Body Language": A New Perspective' (*Enlightened Groves: Essays in Honour of Professor Zenzo Suzuki*, 1996), the late Donald Greene, summarizes nicely what happens when we let personal biography take precedence over artistic achievement. We wind up asking:

> How does the writer measure up to our own moral and social standards? Does one really approve of the existence of such a person? Would one really have cared to have the author as a friend or even as an occasional companion? Would he have been a congenial member of one's household, a suitable associate for one's spouse and children? . . . The worst consequence of this attitude is that it distracts or excuses us from paying attention to what is the only reason for [the artist] being remembered at all – the fact that he has a great deal to say to us, in remarkably effective language, concerning matters that are and will continue to be of prime importance to the human race.

Although some may disapprove of the shattering of the Larkin icon, Neil Covey says in *Contemporary Literature* (1994) that the Larkin biography and letters 'should result in a healthy trend toward criticism of Larkin and his work that acknowledges him for what he was – a deep-feeling, complicated, contrary, contradictory, not easily pigeonholed artist.'

I think Covey and others are absolutely right when they say that complaints about Larkin's viciousness and misogyny say more about the reviewer and his own agenda than they do about Larkin. Whatever one thinks of Larkin's life, it cannot be denied that he created exquisite poems that will last, and Motion does better than anyone I know in exploring some of the raw material from which those poems were fashioned. One of Motion's most interesting arguments about Larkin is that he needed the pain of his life in order to work, a condition that Richard Rhodes describes well in *How to Write: Advice and Reflections* (1995): 'writing is always a healing process because the function of creation is always, *always*, the alleviation of pain – the writer's, first of all, and then the pain of those who read what he has written. Imagination is compassionate.'

Clearly, compassion is not on the minds of those readers and critics for whom the publication of Larkin's *Selected Letters* and Motion's *A Writer's Life* were upsetting, disquieting, even disllusioning. As John Updike notes with keen insight, however, 'The trouble with literary biographies, perhaps, is that they mainly testify to the long worldly corruption of a life, as documented deeds and days and disappointments pile up, and cannot convey the unearthly human innocence that attends, in the perpetual present tense of living, the self that seems the real one' (*The New Yorker*, 26 June 1995).

Larkin's books will survive, of course, and it will be because of that unearthly human innocence, that authenticity in what he wrote rather than anything that *we* have written about *him*.

Samuel Johnson's admonishment to a lady anxious for an introduction to some writer then much in the limelight remains true: 'Dearest Madam,' he wrote, 'you had better let it alone; the best part of every author is in general to be found in his book, I assure you.'

9

Devouring of the Printed Page

ANN THWAITE

It is a Saturday afternoon in late October and I am alone at home, thinking I should get down to writing an essay about books, which I promised long ago. I agreed to do it presumably because the subtext is close to my heart. I do indeed have a passion for books and a distrust of 'information technology', which is as much to do with my technical incompetence as anything else.

I have spent a good deal of my life encouraging children (my own and literally hundreds of other people's) to read. I will say more about that later on, but for the moment I am here in a field sitting in a canvas chair on a warm autumn afternoon, and I have decided to read, not write. Years ago, nearly twenty years ago, we planted the trees that surround me – beeches behind my chair, some despised cypresses a neighbour was discarding to my right. I remember thinking (noting where the sun fell in the afternoon) that this would be a good sheltered corner for reading when the trees grew; and now they are grown, and the children have grown up too and gone, and I realise with a pang that I have *never* before today brought a canvas chair to this nearby field and read a book.

The sky is cloudless, some bird above me makes a curious chattering sound, and every now and again a golden leaf drops from the birch in front of me to the grass beneath it. Piles of mown grass left by the tractor's pre-winter cut stud the field. The piles should be raked to allow the wild flowers (or even the grass itself) to flourish next spring. There are nettles springing up by the stream where my grandchildren will play next summer. Something should be done about them. There are branches lying around (since the last strong wind) which should be gathered for kindling the winter's log fires. Back in the house, on my desk, there are always letters waiting to be answered, telephone calls that should be made. There are always things that seem more important than reading for pleasure.

Reading for *work*, of course, is another matter, and I do that all the time, but not in a canvas chair in a corner of a field. I will say more about that too later on, but now I am going to read.

The cat, surprised to find me in a field that usually seems more his than ours, came and sat on my knee as I read, licking the hand holding the book, warming my thighs as the sun went down behind the far trees. I read, and it was the most recent book I had bought – brief, current, inviting, the easiest book on the Booker shortlist: *The Essence of the Thing* by Madeleine St John. It was very suitable for reading at one draught. It was swift and stylish and thought-provoking. I'd picked it up in Dillons in Piccadilly late at night a few days earlier, reduced in price (a 'loss leader' perhaps), and, thrown in with it, a free cassette of presentations by all the Booker shortlist authors. In theory I disapprove of the ending of the Net Book Agreement, which means that booksellers in Britain are now allowed to charge what they like for their books. I know it is hard for independent booksellers, struggling to make any profit at all, to have the current bestsellers reduced in price by the big chains, Waterstones, Dillons, Books Etc. But as a *buyer*, rather than as a writer whose books are not likely to be reduced and seem now even more expensive than they did before, I can't help being glad to be able to acquire from time to time a new novel for less than the price of an Indian supper. It can be an impulse buy rather than the result of considered thought.

I find myself often protesting when people complain of the price of books. I remember chiding a Tory Minister for the Arts on this point once, long ago, at a Booker Prize dinner. He had said (incredibly, to a writer whose earnings some years would hardly keep her agent in ink cartridges for his fax machine) how much he regretted that books were so expensive. Why is it that people will cheerfully sign away a huge sum on a credit card for a meal or theatre tickets, but baulk at the cost of a book? Twice recently I have paid the price of a fat biography for a theatre ticket and found myself craning round other people's heads to see a disappointing play, with afterwards nothing to hold in one's hand and go through again to revisit the good bits and to try and decide why it was disappointing.

Choosing books that *won't* disappoint is not always easy, but it is always easier than choosing plays. A new play is usually something of what used to be called 'a pig in a poke', a phrase apparently first popularised by Chaucer in the Reeve's Tale. 'Poke' is an extremely interesting word. It is, of course, a love of language, and what it can do, that lies behind the passion for books. In the case of 'poke' a happy hour can be spent reading the eight and a half columns (if one goes as far as the related 'poky') in the *Oxford English Dictionary*. I particularly like the phrase 'poke-shakings' which can be used ('fig.') of the youngest child in a family or indeed the smallest of a litter of pigs, from the original meaning 'the last portion of meal etc shaken out of a sack.' In our 1933 edition of the thirteen volumes there are several quotations from 'Miss Yonge', e.g. 'I suppose she is not much of a lady, living *poked* up there', from *Lads and Lasses of Langley*, 1881. Even admirers (and there are many) of Charlotte M. Yonge's *Countess Kate* may not have read about those Lads and Lasses. Which leads me to think of those huge numbers of out-of-print books, much enjoyed in their day, which now throng the shelves of secondhand booksellers.

I have a fantasy (and fantasies are by their nature impossible) of a year's moratorium on new books, when publishers are allowed only to reprint the best books from the past. Of course tastes and fashions change, and thousands (even millions) of out-of-print books do not deserve a new lease of life; but other thousands (or at least many hundreds) are as readable and relevant today as they ever were. One of my happiest achievements was finding a publisher (Scolar, now Ashgate) who was prepared to let me edit a collection of Edmund Gosse's essays about people he had known, including Walt Whitman, Christina Rossetti, Hardy, James, Browning. These 'portraits from life' had been scattered in a dozen long out-of-print books of essays with fusty titles, such as *Critical Kit-Kats* and *Some Diversions of a Man of Letters*.

Robert Louis Stevenson – himself the subject of the first portrait in my collection – once told Gosse to 'see as many people as you can and make a book of them before you die. That will be a living book, upon my word'. Gosse certainly 'saw' huge numbers of people; he wrote mainly about writers. For, as he said, what had possessed him all his life was 'an intense love of books and of the history of authors. The indulgence of this passion has been the joy of my life'.

Edmund Gosse certainly had a passion for books, but he also had a passion for life and for friendship; and it is this that makes him continue to be worth reading, unlike his contemporary George Saintsbury, who preferred 'conversation by books' to the conversation of men and women. (He seems to have liked women, but would always rather write to them than see them.) In her biography of him, Dorothy Richardson Jones offers a sample list of his reading: 'all of Diderot: Pickwick, Peacock, *Wuthering Heights*, *The Antiquary*, Southey's *The Doctor*, Jane Austen, Thackeray and so forth all reread once a year; *The Earthly Paradise* read twenty times with unfading delight; *Gulliver* a hundred times; three hundred volumes of Gautier; all of the *Anti-Jacobin*; *The Anatomy of Melancholy* read through twice . . . '

The legend was, moreover, that he read a French novel every morning before breakfast. Edmund Wilson apparently called Saintsbury a literary glutton, and looked in his private life for the morbid roots of this disorder. It certainly seems to us sad if someone appears to have loved Boswell's *Life of Johnson* better than he loved his wife, but it could be that he thought it fitting to write of his love for the book and *not* to write of his love of a woman.

After a reading list such as Saintsbury's, we may feel we can hardly claim to be passionate readers at all, as we attempt or neglect to keep up with the latest best-sellers, the books everyone talks about (*Wild Swans*, *Longitude*, *A Brief History of Time*, the new Margaret Atwood or Ian McEwan), and neglect our regular rereading of the books we know we care about. For writers, whose friends are so often other writers, there is also the huge category of books by friends. How often do we mutter to each other: 'I'm sorry, I haven't got round to it yet.' What a pleasure it is when a friend *does* read one of our books, and loves it, and takes the trouble to write and say so. These are the best kind of fan letter, treasured particularly because the writer knows how many hundreds of long silent hours have gone into the writing.

There was a time when I prided myself that I reread all Jane Austen's novels every couple of years. Was it that in those days the house was not as crammed as it is now with books I have not yet read? Sometimes a visitor, who would not recognize that 'books do furnish a room' (or even have heard of Anthony Powell), stares bewildered at our overflowing bookshelves and asks, 'Have you really read them all?'; and naturally one has to admit that one hasn't. Even so, in the course of a year, it is amazing how many hundreds of them have been handled for one reason or another – and how many more we have acquired.

One thing that gives me great pleasure is keeping track of my own daughters' reading. One of them has read *Tom Jones*, not once but twice (once more than I have) and *Daniel Deronda*, which for some reason I never have. And I delight in the fact that it is more likely to be Thomas Hardy than John Grisham they choose for plane journeys and beach reading. But they are not locked into the past, and at least two of them are better read in contemporary fiction than I am.

Which brings me back to the subject of children and reading, for my daughters were, of course, children once. I see a close relation between what children read and their later lives, not only as readers but as people. Readers can be quiet and enjoy themselves in solitude; readers have lively minds (did not someone once say 'Reading is to the mind what exercise is to the body?'); readers are never bored. The same, I can hear someone saying, is true of devotees of the internet. But contrast the sight of a child absorbed in a book and one hopping about on the worldwide web. Contrast, too, any day on public transport (for instance, the London Underground) the sight of a passenger reading a book and one flicking through a newspaper. It is absorption, not surfing, that brings happiness.

Gore Vidal was reported recently as saying that American students 'don't know how to read a novel'. Saul Bellow sees a time when the serious novel will be almost entirely usurped by cinema, television and cyberspace. Who will have time to dwell on irony and allusion, on cadence and character? On public transport in England the novel seems to be alive and well, if something of a minority habit. But it was not long ago that I saw two people (not travelling together but in the same railway carriage) reading Zola novels. And I cherish a recent memory of a fellow passenger on the Underground laughing over a novel and totally unaware that everyone else in the compartment was trying to see what he was reading. (It was Tom Sharpe.)

Two of my favourite quotations relate to reading. They are both well known but bear repetition. There will always be someone coming across them for the first time. It was Dr Johnson who said, 'The only end of writing is to enable the readers better to enjoy life, or better to endure it'. It was Graham Greene who stressed the importance of early reading: 'The influence of early books is profound. So much of the future lies on the shelves: early reading has more influence on conduct than any religious teaching'. I suppose this is one reason I have spent much of my life concerned with children's books and with helping children find the books that will turn them into readers. For twenty years I had a children's library in my house, and well over a thousand children came through our river door and into the book room. As Ted Hughes once put it: 'Imaginative literature does have a magical effect on people's minds and on their ultimate behaviour.' How important, it seems, that children's minds should be fed with nourishing food, with constant reminders that the world is an exciting place, to be explored and relished for all its dangers. They need to meet, not villains to be zapped on a playstation, but some versions of the sort of world they are going to meet in real life. But they will thrive on happy endings, at least until they have achieved some sort of maturity.

I am writing this just after the closure of the Round Reading Room in the British Museum in Bloomsbury. It is a place of particular resonance for me. Not only have I spent hundreds of hours reading there myself, but it was the place where young Edmund Gosse, one of my beloved 'subjects', started out on his career, arriving aged seventeen in 1867 to work there as a 'Junior Assistant or Transcriber'. At that time 'great laxity prevailed'. Only a small amount of work was 'demanded from the slaves by slave drivers even lazier than themselves'. Cricket was practised in remote galleries; others 'cultivated the jew's harp'. Gosse's 'own diversion was reading, ceaseless devouring of the printed page . . . Through the long silent afternoons, immersed in the curious odour of slowly decaying calf-skin, I would stand in the Upper Gallery of the King's Library or among the Garrick Plays, absorbing with ceaseless appetite the obscurer parts of seventeenth century literature'.

Miserable readers have recently made huge statements about the closure of the Round Reading Room in Bloomsbury. 'The separation of Library and Museum, of mind from body, is an intellectual tragedy', wrote Neal Ascherson. 'Placed where it was, as the navel of the museum, the library symbolised the unity of abstract and concrete, of all that human beings had thought with all that they had made'. Readers may learn to love the new British Library in St Pancras, but what chills the blood is the thought of the fate of the Round Reading Room itself. It is to be an 'interactive information centre' for the British Museum and will open in the year 2000 with, one imagines, serried ranks of computers on the blue leather desks. The chill is because this seems to say that nothing is sacred, that everything can change. Not everything. Surely the desks must be listed and preserved – with the bookrests and penholders designed by Antonio Panizzi 140 years ago? I've always wondered what exactly it was Algernon Swinburne cut his head on when he fainted at one of those desks in 1868. It was Gosse's first sight of his hero, 'our greatest living poet', carried out of the reading room with blood in his bright hair.

Who reads Swinburne now? Who indeed has heard of Swinburne now? (I have tried his name on some clever young and drawn a blank.) But the poems remain to be discovered by some fresh reader in the new millennium. The words in books don't disappear as easily as words wiped from a screen. Indeed I have on my shelves an edition published as recently as 1982, edited by L. M. Findlay, who wrote in his introduction: 'The rehabilitation of Swinburne is inevitably an uncertain enterprise.' Was there really a time (as Gosse reported) when the young men of Cambridge joined hands and shouted 'Dolores'? Certainly Swinburne is difficult reading for anyone not steeped in classical and biblical imagery.

The more we read the more we can appreciate what we read. As a biographer, I have read, as well as much prose, not only Swinburne and Tennyson but many other nineteenth-century poets, who astonishingly were too modern to be part of the university syllabus when I was at Oxford in the 1950s. Writing a biography is above all an excuse for reading – even, sometimes, novels in the morning, which used to be considered the height of decadence. And not only books of course, but, even more delightfully, thousands of unpublished letters, some of which indeed have not been read by anyone else since that long-ago day when the first recipient took the letter out of its envelope.

I am a compulsive writer. When I am not writing a book, I write notes, of course, but also letters and a journal – and occasionally essays such as this. But if, heaven forfend, I had to choose between reading and writing, I immediately think I would choose reading. I mentioned the fantasy of a year when publishers would only reprint books from the past. I have another fantasy – of a year when I could do nothing but read. I would read all those books I have always wanted to read, and I would read again, with renewed pleasure, many books I have loved and half-forgotten. And yet, as I write this, I think as the historian J. R. Green once wrote: 'Anyone can read! The difficulty is to write – to make something'. That must be the real joy.

10

Discovering *Jane Eyre*
CATHERINE PETERS

A few months ago I spent a morning with a group of young people, sixteen and seventeen years old, all studying English literature, all intelligent, well-motivated students intending to go to university. When I asked what they read for pleasure, I discovered they didn't. Only one or two had recently read a book not on the school syllabus. When I gave them some poems to read and discuss, a universal groan went up. 'We don't like poetry', they chorused. Evidently the phenomenon of 'pop' oral poetry had not yet reached their school.

I was rocked back on my heels by this experience, which seemed to confirm all the gloomy forebodings of the end of reading. When I went away and thought about it, I realized that these young people were literate, though not in my way, at home in the world of electronic communication as I shall never be. But books were for them a means to an end, not a pleasure, still less a passion.

In the 1930s I grew up in a very different world. We had the radio, and, as a very occasional treat, the cinema. I went to ballet matinees more often than to films. But there were no computers, no television or video, no CDs or tapes, no faxes or internet. Parents worried about their children's reading habits, even then – would we be seduced away from books by comics, or cartoon films? – and some children were of course more eager and efficient natural readers than others. But it was rare to come across a middle-class child who never read a book for pleasure. Now, in our post-Gutenberg world there are so many enticing alternatives.

Yet all small children love being read to, and many pre-adolescent children still love reading. There is so much anxiety about encouraging the reading habit in children nowadays, that perhaps the sheer sensual pleasure of the book as object is overlooked. You can't take a computer or television screen up a tree, or smuggle it into bed to read by torchlight under the covers. It is cold and unrewarding to touch and smell. Television may have a hypnotic effect, but I have seen a ten-month-old baby's attention held for twenty-five minutes by picture-books, as she turned over the pages, giving little exclamations of delight. The world of the small child is, as Virginia Woolf remembered in 'A Sketch of the Past', a wonderful confused mass: 'sounds indistinguishable from sights . . . I am hardly aware of myself, but only of the sensation.' Books can become a part of that world of sensation.

Before I developed a passion for reading, still less a passion for literature, indeed ever since I can remember, I have had 'a passion for books'; books as objects. I was vividly conscious of the smell and feeling of the books I handled, and I have never lost my pleasure in their physical existence. I love to feel a book's weight in the hand, sniff the faintly acrid scent of old paper; the wet-emulsion-paint smell of new print; the Rolls-Royce whiff of leather. The rough or smooth texture of a cloth cover, the incised, elaborate decoration of the Andrew Lang fairy books, green, blue, purple, grey and crimson, were an excitement in themselves. To this day to wrinkle one's nose at a book and finger its pages, to feel the shiny paper of the dustwrapper, is a pre-emptive pleasure as evocative as the sight of its print or illustrations. I am incapable of throwing a book away, no matter how trivial or unsatisfactory I have found it. Even when its cover is loose, its pages fluttering to the ground, grimy and virtually illegible, putting it in the dustbin seems like murdering a family pet. I do sometimes, reluctantly, *give* a book away, only to long for it back next day.

I am not a bibliophile or collector; though I buy both new and second-hand books compulsively I don't haunt the auction rooms for first editions, or have my library bound in uniform calfskin. It is, as it should be for an adult, what a book contains that matters most to me now, even if I take a clandestine sniff at a new volume, or rub my finger over the spine of an old favourite. Great care is taken, rightly, to make books for little children attractive. The formats are impressively big or delectably small, the print is large and the paper thick, the pictures well drawn and colourful. But what of the next step? How are children to make the transition to reading for content, when the pleasure of the object becomes irrelevant? Even children who do enjoy reading now often feel that the books that adults read are formidable, too difficult, or too boring ever to be tackled. It is amazing to remember that Victorian children read the novels of Scott for pleasure.

My ten-year-old granddaughter, a passionate reader, said defiantly, 'I'm never going to read grown-up books.' I tried to erode the distinction by pointing out that some of her favourite books, *Little Women* and its sequels, or Mary Norton's *Borrowers* series, were also read and enjoyed by grown-ups. But her conviction that there was a great gulf between children's books and the adult world of literature made me wonder if the immense pleasure in reading and being read to that is offered by the current profusion of beautifully produced children's books of high quality must be left behind with childhood. Sometimes, when I look at the shelves of audio-books in my local bookshop I wonder whether the next generation but one will read, in the old-fashioned sense, at all.

Such gloomy thoughts aroused memories of my own childhood. I realized that though I devoured print avidly, reading advertisement hoardings or bus tickets rather than nothing at all, for a long time I made no attempt to explore the books which filled my home. Like my granddaughter, I was happy with children's books, most of them supplied by my elders, supplemented by a comic, usually *Tiger Tim*. To get this I had laboriously to save my Saturday penny for a fortnight. It meant missing every other episode of the serials, which didn't seem to matter much. The comic-strip format, and the sense that it was, though not forbidden, not approved of, were what attracted me. Perhaps we should try forbidding the books we want children to read, or at least make them less easily accessible? When I began to think about how I made the transition from nursery reading to a more sophisticated and exploratory stage, I don't remember a teacher in the classroom; I remember Aunt Alice.

My mother didn't believe in too much school. It was enough for her that I could read at five, and I did not start school until I was six. She didn't value the 'playing about' that went on at my school in the afternoon; the painting, craft, gym, games and communal activities that I would have dearly loved to share were not what she sent me there for. I was later on allowed Brownies once a week, which involved the heady pleasure of school lunch: thick gravy, custard made with Bird's Custard powder instead of eggs; such things were never known at home.

On Wednesday afternoons, while my class-mates played netball, my mother and I went to have tea with Aunt Alice. She was really my great-aunt, and very important in my life, being one of my few close relations. My grandparents were dead, my only brother, nine years older, away at boarding school. Aunt Alice lived in Westbourne Park Gardens, in a first-floor room with two balconies, in a genteel boarding-house run by Miss Armstrong with the help of a tall, gaunt parlourmaid called Rose. When Rose opened the door to us on Wednesdays at four, wearing her blue afternoon uniform, with a frilled apron and cap, I couldn't help thinking she looked like a very, very nice elderly cart-horse, particularly when she smiled, showing large, regular false teeth. She would always show us up to the first floor, though it was hardly likely we would have forgotten the way, to Aunt Alice's cosy over-furnished room.

By the time I remember her, Aunt Alice was completely crippled with arthritis, and could only go out in a bath-chair. Her hands were so badly knotted and swollen that she could hardly hold a teacup, and she lived almost totally confined to that one room for about ten years, until she died in 1943. She refused to be taken down to a shelter during the London blitz, and sat there alone, unable to move or do anything to help herself if the house had been hit. She wrote to my mother with typical understatement, 'I'm so glad you are not here, Helen. It really is not very pleasant at the moment.' But she was by no means cut off from the world outside. She was a most lively and amusing old lady who kept up with world affairs, read all the latest books from the Times Library, and had almost more visitors than she wanted. She was the strong link in a tenuous chain of cousins, second cousins, cousins once- and twice-removed, and she and my mother would spend the afternoon deep in gossip about the adventures and misdeeds of these distant relations, none of them more than names to me.

After tea was over, and the tray taken away by Rose, the white cloth taken off the blue serge one and folded up and put away, boredom, that inescapable doppelgänger of my childhood, rapidly overtook me. Once I had explored, yet again, the various fragile ornaments in the room, asked for, and been refused permission to go out on the balcony (my mother was convinced I would fall to my death) I would sit on the floor behind the sofa by the small bookcase in the corner of the room, forgotten for an hour or so, and see what I could find.

The top shelf was full of works of piety. There was a Bible in limp black leather covers, with maps of the Holy Land, and the collected works of Mary Baker Eddy, of which I can only remember the *Christian Science Manual* and *Science and Health: With a Key to the Scriptures*. My aunt, in spite of her arthritis, was a devout Christian Scientist, as was my grandmother, her sister, who had died of cancer after years of pain. It didn't seem to matter to either of them that their faith had been noticeably lacking in tangible results. Perhaps they got a secret satisfaction from a sect headed by a woman, after their years of servitude as dutiful Victorian daughters, from which Alice never escaped until the death of her parents.

The bottom shelf of the bookcase had books kept especially for me. There were A. A. Milne, *The Tale of Peter Rabbit*, and some others which might have been found in any collection of children's books in the 1930s. But I soon graduated from them to richer food. Very early editions of *Alice in Wonderland* and *Through the Looking Glass*, inscribed to 'dearest Alice on her eighth birthday, from her loving brother George' kept me going for a long time. I also discovered *Sara Crewe: or What Happened at Miss Minchin's*, one of Frances Hodgson Burnett's best children's stories, unusual for its day in its total identification with the oppressed child against the cruelty of adults.

I must have been nearly eight when, bored by the prospect of rereading the stories I knew so well, I began to explore the 'grown-up' books on the middle shelf. Here I found an enchanting book by Eiluned Lewis, *Dew on the Grass*. Thinly disguised as fiction, it is an account of her childhood with her brothers and sisters in the Welsh border country. The world she described seemed to me as remote and beautiful as a dream, and I was astonished when I discovered, a few years ago, that Eiluned Lewis was still alive. It is still one of my favourite books (I have Aunt Alice's copy). This recreation of a child's world, written by an adult for adults, made a perfect bridge between children's and adult reading.

But the book on the middle shelf which dramatically marked the transition was *Jane Eyre*, which I read when I was eight. A 'Pocket Edition' published by Smith, Elder in 1888, it has the most forbidding format of any book I had ever attempted. The marbled green covers were unattractive, the print was small, the book, though almost as small as *Peter Rabbit*, was inches thick and had

Catherine Peters

no pictures. Yet from the first sentence,'There was no possibility of taking a walk that day', I was hooked.

The impact on an unsophisticated child of Jane's story was almost literally stunning. The early chapters of the book, in which Jane is treated in a way that reinforced the lesson of *Sara Crewe* – that life is arbitrary in its favours, that the strong and rich tyrannize over the weak and poor, and that children suffer at the hands of adults for inadequate and shameful reasons – have never lost the power they had for me then. I felt, though I knew rationally that it was impossible, that these chapters had been written by a child – no adult could have understood a child's feelings so completely. I vividly remember, too, the account of Jane's escape from Rochester, when she begs for the burnt porridge that is being thrown out for the pigs. My struggles with food had been quite the opposite; it was always being thrust at me when I didn't want it. The hair prickled on my neck as the reality of hunger was brought home to me for the first time.

Of course there was much in the story that went over my head. I was a naive and uncritical reader, who read literally; symbolism meant nothing to me. I didn't bother to puzzle over the parts that were difficult, but galloped ahead, fortunately not interrupted by any conscientious adult trying to explain it to me.

A couple of years later, Aunt Alice sent me copies of *Bleak House* and *David Copperfield* for my tenth birthday and Christmas. These started me on Dickens, and after that the distinction between children's books and adult books ceased to have any significance. By then the war had started, and my London life had been exchanged for the isolation of a house in the far West Country. There were even fewer alternatives to reading, and I read everything I could get hold of, from bound volumes of *Punch*, to Jane Austen, to 1930s detective novels.

I saw Aunt Alice once more, four years later. My brother and I went to tea with her during his last leave before he went to India, on his way to the Burmese jungle where he was killed. We took her a bunch of anemones, a flower I always associate with her. Everything in Westbourne Park Gardens seemed exactly the same. Rose and Miss Armstrong were a little older, and I poured out the tea and talked, taking my mother's place, rather than retreating behind the sofa. Aunt Alice was as interested in our lives as ever, and not perceptibly more fragile. She was over eighty, but to a child anyone over sixty is very old, and she hadn't changed for me.

It may seem strange that the weekly visits to this gentle old lady should have been so important in developing my love of literature. But there was something about those long Wednesday afternoons, the boredom, and the lack of choice which made it necessary to go on with whatever I found, even if it was too difficult for me, which made the books I read there key ones, which stuck in my memory. Would unimportant books have stayed with me in the same way? I don't remember a word of Mary Baker Eddy, though I did sometimes have a go at her, in desperation. Nor did I do more than glance at the Bible; though I did (little hypocrite that I was) ask Aunt Alice for a Bible of my own as a sixth birthday present, to her delight. Nowadays children are not expected to tolerate boredom and stay quiet while their elders talk, but perhaps we can craftily devise strategies to help them discover for themselves the delights of reading. I hope my granddaughter will be lucky enough to find, without well-meaning adult interference, the book that is her magic door into 'grown-up books'; as I found *Jane Eyre*.

11

The Radiant Way and After
MARGARET DRABBLE

The first book I remember reading was called *Tot and the Cat*. It had a limp grey cloth cover and crude black and white illustrations and a text of great dullness. I loved it. It was very cheap. I read it again and again. I cannot recall the story line, but I can remember the excitement of the way signs continued to turn into words before my eyes. They did it every time. The book was there, for me, and I could read it whenever I wanted. This seemed a miracle, and seems so still. I was three years old, according to my mother, when this miracle occurred, but I think she may have exaggerated my precocity. In later years she told me that for her there was a pathos in watching me read *Tot and the Cat* over and over again, for it was a wartime reading production on poor paper, and she could remember the pre-war days of lavishly illustrated and brightly coloured children's books. She was a little saddened that I was so pleased by so little.

I remember also my first primer, in The *Radiant Way* series, a title which I borrowed to ironic purpose for one of my recent novels. I recall lines of text – 'Pat can sing. Mother can sing. Sing to mother, Pat.' This too had a magic beyond its surface meaning. (My mother could not sing, and neither can I.) And from these first steps I embarked on that radiant way and now I am unhappy unless I have a book about my person. I carry one in my handbag, in my pocket. I read at bus stops, on aeroplanes, at the supermarket checkout, in bed, on the beach. I fear being trapped in a lift or detained in prison without a book. I need a book as a chaperon in a restaurant, and reading while eating alone with a good book is one of the great pleasures of life.

It will follow from that statement that I am not a bibliophile, and pay little respect to fine bindings, fine paper and fine print. One of the rarest items in my own bibliography is a piece I wrote

in 1966 for the catalogue of an antiquarian bookseller friend: it
was entitled 'Wordsworth's Butter Knife', and it alluded to the
reading habits of Wordsworth and his friend Southey. Southey,
or so De Quincey tells us, was proud of his many thousand
volumes and manuscripts in English, Spanish and Portuguese:
they were 'fine copies, and decorated externally with a reasonable
elegance, so as to make them in harmony with the other embellishments of the room.' Wordsworth's few hundred books, in contrast,
were ill bound or not bound at all, stained, torn, and mutilated
by his children; they were kept in a 'little homely painted bookcase' by the fireplace. 'Wordsworth lived in the open air: Southey
in his library, which Coleridge used to call his wife. Southey had
particularly elegant habits (Wordsworth called them finical) in
the use of books. Wordsworth, on the other hand, was so negli-
gent, and so self-indulgent in the same case, that as Southey,
laughing, expressed it to me some years afterwards, when I was
staying at Greta Hall on a visit – "To introduce Wordsworth into
one's library, is like letting a bear into a tulip garden."'

De Quincey continues his tale with a description of Wordsworth's
visiting him for tea and buttered toast in his cottage at Grasmere,
and spying on the shelf the collected works of Edmund Burke.
Wordsworth took down a volume, and found it 'unfortunately'
uncut: he at once reached for the butter knife 'and tore his way
into the heart of the volume with this knife that left its greasy
honours behind it upon every page: and are they not there to
this day?' ('William Wordsworth and Robert Southey', *Tait's
Edinburgh Magazine*, July 1839).

I have always been on Wordsworth's side, and think of him
on the rare occasions when I find myself confronted in the Reading
Room of the British Library with an uncut text. Readers are
requested to return an uncut volume to the Centre Desk for
professional assistance, and not to hack at it themselves with fingers
or pencil: this I dutifully do, but I can understand Wordsworth's
impatience, his eager desire to get at the words within. There is
a silent pathos in a book which has waited patiently, unread, for
two hundred years: one such was John Cunningham's *Poems chiefly
pastoral*, published in 1766, which I requested in the Reading Room
when compiling and revising entries for the Fifth Edition of the
Oxford Companion to English Literature. Poor Cunningham! He was
the author of one successful farce, and earned his living as an
actor, though he was not a very good actor. He published this

one volume of verse. Would he not have preferred his poems to be covered with butter rather than to remain unread? And I am only slightly ashamed of the reprimand I received from a reader sitting at the next seat in the British Library, who told me off for forcing back the spine of a rare Forrest Reid novel – clearly nobody had ever opened it before, and a certain amount of pressure had to be applied to make the pages stay open at all.

Angus Wilson, whose biography I have recently written, was for some years Deputy Superintendent of the Reading Room, and he had many tales of readers' misdemeanours: one of his favourites was his account of the woman who, when challenged for eating oranges at her desk, retorted that she was not eating them, she was squeezing the juice of them onto the books. But Angus himself, at home, was not a great respecter of books as objects. Like many impassioned readers and teachers, he annotated his library heavily, with marginalia, underlinings, exclamation marks. Each teaching copy is a mixture of commentary on and dialogue with the author. Graham Greene, I believe, was of similar habits, and so of course am I. So is my daughter, and when I come upon a book which has previously been read by her I feel I am enjoying a conversation with her. The first time I read *War and Peace* I read it in her copy, and I thoroughly enjoyed her at times caustic comments: her admiration was tempered by remarks like 'Repetition!' or 'Bathos!', though she also bestows a few approving ticks. These much-read volumes have a history in time, and they tell stories beyond their own.

I even enjoy the contact one may have with other unknown readers through library books: I've just read Claire Tomalin's theatre biography, *Mrs Jordan's Profession*, in which some previous borrower has naughtily coloured in with red ink many of the 'O's. Was there a pattern to the inking, I wondered? Most of them seemed to cluster in the names of titled ladies. Had we a republican at work? Or was this more *une vrai Histoire D'O*, full of sexual innuendo? And is it possible that librarians, appointed as preservers and defenders, nourish a secret desire to vandalize their charges? Of all the revelations in Philip Larkin's life as told by poet Andrew Motion none was more surprising than his secret penchant for defacing books – the last bad habit one might have expected in a poet-librarian.

I buy more and more books, partly for the pleasure of being able to write in them without guilt, but I am still a heavy user of public and specialist libraries. I recall my first library ticket as one of the great passports to life, and am enchanted to find my grandchildren as devoted to Oxford Public Libraries as I was to our little branch in East Hardwick, near Pontefract. I must have been about five when I was allowed to take my first books home, and one I remember with an intense and inexplicable delight. It was called *The Curious Lobster*, by Richard W. Hatch, and I was charmed by its strange landscapes, its witty creatures. (I have liked crustaceans ever since.) What was it doing in a Children's Library in a tiny village in mining country in South Yorkshire, and why did I love it so much? I had no knowledge then that it was set in America – just as I never realized that other early classic favourites like *What Katy Did* or the less distinguished Sue Barton 'nurse' series by Helen Dore Boylston were American. And I discovered only the other day that Munro Leaf's *Ferdinand the Bull* had also crossed the Atlantic. All was strange, and all was wonderful. There were no books about the kind of life I led, the kind of world I lived in, but at that age this bothered me not at all. It was only much, much later that I started to need books to which I could relate, which would teach me how to live.

Children have extraordinary capacities for digesting the indigestible. In the summer of 1995, while sorting out the shelves and cupboards before moving house, I came across a school prize which I was given at that first small school, in 1944, when I was five, inscribed 'For Good Progress' by the headmistress, Miss Royston. It was a version of *Les Malheurs du Sophie* (1864), by the Comtesse de Ségur, translated as *The Misfortunes of Sophy*, by Honor and Edgar Skinner, and published in 1943 by Williams and Norgate Ltd of 36 Great Russell Street. Rereading this work now, I see that it is most unsuitable matter for a small child: not quite in the category of Foxe's *Book of Martyrs*, with which Victorian children whiled away their Sunday afternoons, but in its own way alarming enough. Poor Sophy, unlike her little cousin Paul, is a child much given to bad behaviour: she steals sweets, torments and causes the death of a donkey, and drowns her pet tortoise, actions which provoke both reprimand and remorse. The illustrations (three of them full colour plates, unusual in those days of austerity) have a certain charm, but the tales themselves are punitive. I must have perused them many times, and taken them to heart: were they in part responsible for my early and sometimes crushing sense of guilt? As a child, I always felt I was in the wrong, even when I wasn't. And, ten years later, at fifteen, how closely I identified with another fictitious naughty child, who even shared my own name – Maggie Tulliver, in George Eliot's *The Mill on the Floss*, seemed to have been created for me alone.

Looking back now at the misadventures of Sophie de Réan and Maggie Tulliver, I see that they both committed the same crime: both were responsible for the deaths of animals entrusted to their care. (Maggie, perhaps uncharacteristically for so sensitive a child, neglects the rabbits which her brother Tom has left in her charge, and they die of starvation.) This crime struck me, at the time, as very terrible, nor do I think that I myself could ever have been as carelessly callous: whenever any of my pet creatures died, as creatures must, I suffered intense and disproportionate grief. I wept long with Adolphus the carp and Mittens the cat, and I still wake from dreams in which I have forgotten to feed a kitten, a goldfish, or even the dog which I have never owned. Is this recurrent nightmare a tribute to the narrative power of the Comtesse de Ségur? Did I feel guilt as well as loss?

Our early reading stays with us and affects us in ways we may not know. Angus Wilson was lastingly overshadowed by a children's book he read as a small boy, called *Golliwogg's Adventures at the North Pole*, by Bertha Upton: he had forgotten both title and author, though he mentioned its effect in his autobiographical Ewing lectures in California (printed as *The Wild Garden*, 1963). When I tracked down a copy of the book, in the British Library, I could see exactly why it had affected him, and I wish that I had been able to include a colour print of Golliwogg's frightened and frightening face as he tramped through the eerie frozen wastes.

As we grow older our needs change, and we seek different satisfactions from books. Looking back over half a century of books, I can see distinct phases of need. There was, for example, that strange interlude when I was in my mid teens and my mother, in her fifties, was undergoing some kind of mental stress – a form of agoraphobic depression, I now think, though I could not have put a name to it at the time. Her solace was books: she turned to them (much as Angus Wilson's Mrs Eliot, in *The Middle Age of Mrs Eliot*, turns to them) for comfort. At this low period she read mostly English middle-class detective stories from the library, of which she would devour several a week, and I would read them too as she handed them on: we read our way through Dorothy L. Sayers, Margery Allingham, Patricia Wentworth, Ngaio

Marsh, Christiana Brand, 'Nicholas Blake' (alias Cecil Day-Lewis),
Carter Dickson, Dickson Carr, and many others whose names I
have forgotten. She read to escape from herself, and I too read
to escape from her, but those light novels also taught me many
of the facts of life – I learned about sex and its many variations,
about social blunders, about the names of cocktails which in life
I never saw. It cannot be a coincidence that when my mother
died, quite suddenly and unexpectedly, I took myself off to the
holiday cottage in Dorset which I had booked for her annual
summer fortnight with me, and read my way with great pleasure
through an Omnibus Edition of Margery Allingham. These silly,
snobbish stories took me back to a time of mixed grief and hope,
of long boring afternoons in the garden or an armchair, when
my life was all before me, and hers, she felt, behind her. (She
recovered from this phase, and moved on, at my sister's prompting,
to Proust, who became one of the passions of her later years.)

We now live in a society where books are so easily obtainable
that we undervalue them. When we find ourselves in parts of
the world where they are scarce, those of us who are addicts
become anxious and fretful. Even non-addicts may discover in
themselves a deep unrecognized need for print. My younger son,
who is what I would call a cryptic reader, found himself reading
all sorts of strange matter while travelling in Australia and the
South Seas: at one point in the bush he was even reduced to
making his way through a second-hand paperback of my novel
The Millstone. (His verdict: 'Not bad, Mum.') I used his experience in a scene in *The Gates of Ivory*, where two young men are
sailing as crew on a rich man's yacht through the Timor Sea:
one of them begs the other, a new arrival on board, for reading
matter: 'I'm not much a reading man, but you kind of get driven
to it, don't you? You haven't got a spare paperback to see me on
my way? I'd do you a swap. I've got a Graham Greene in the
cabin. *The Third Man*. It's a bit short, but it's quite good.'

Eva Hoffman, in *Exit into History* (1993), her account of Eastern
Europe after the fall of the Berlin Wall, addresses a similar theme,
and gives a moving account of the lonely traveller's dependence
on the company of books: hers is the solitude of a writer-observer
who is meeting and interviewing new people nearly every day,
and only in books does she find coherence. Of her stay in Prague,
she writes:

I've run out of reading matter and my need for a book has become quite as urgent as my need for dinner or sleep. Travel apparently restores to one the meaning of literature . . . I begin to understand why travel writers are always alluding to what they've been reading, even as they are scaling a glacier or plunging into a deadly swamp. Faced with the unformed world before me, with the plethora of places, personalities, and accidental encounters, I crave the shapeliness, the ready-made order, of a written world.

So I enter the 'international' bookstore with high hopes. These are soon crushed. The English section features *Treasure Island*, *Robinson Crusoe*, and *Little Women* . . . In my famished state, I buy *Little Women*, which in my Eastern European childhood, I hadn't read, and *Robinson Crusoe*, which I had. At the counter next to me, a middle-aged American tourist is buying *Robinson Crusoe* and *Treasure Island*. His desperation apparently equals mine.

Anyone with a passion for reading (which may, perhaps, be slightly different from a passion for books) will recognize this description, as readers recognize one another. I am one of those who always peers inquisitively at the titles of other people's books, in their homes as shown as on TV, on the underground, on aeroplanes. Some reciprocate. On my way to Canada recently I was as usual furnished with four or five volumes to last the journey, and I noticed that they were attracting the attention of my neighbour, who did not at a first sideways glance look much of a reading man: I found myself trying to conceal from his gaze the jacket and alarming illustrations of my friend Brian Masters' biography of a serial killer, brilliantly entitled *Killing for Company*. Over our meal, all was explained: my travelling companion was a Canadian engineer who worked in the North African desert, six weeks on, six weeks off, and he was forced to read his way through the long desert nights. His favourite author, for whose works he had a true passion, was Jean Auel, a best seller of whom I had then never heard: I was touched by the warmth with which he spoke of her works. She had kept him alive in exile. I bought one or two as a result of his recommendations, and could see what had captured him.

On consideration, I begin to think that what I have is not only a passion for books: it is also a passion for print. Hence my sense of helpless confusion in Japan: if I cannot even read the street signs, I am lost in more senses than one. Images won't suffice: I need words and print. This dependence doesn't fit very easily with my faith that not all our emotions can be conveyed in words – I believe that emotion precedes grammar, and that we can have thoughts without words. But I need print like an addict. I could live without it, perhaps. But I hope I never have to try.

12

Reading My Father

MARY GORDON

As I walk the two blocks from my home to the Columbia library, I remember going to the public library with my father. It was just one room, a large room on the second floor, above a paint store. The librarian was portly, rigidly corseted, except for the doughy flesh on her arms, which was visible when she wore a short-sleeved dress. She was uniformly, constantly displeased. She never looked happy when we took out books. We could tell she would have preferred that the books be left on the shelves, untouched, unopened, only thought about.

My father and I went to the library every Saturday. We climbed the stairs and separated; he went to the adult section, I to the children's. I always felt an anxiety about choosing: I didn't know what the criteria were, and suppose I made the wrong choice? His policy was to let me wander, let me alone, but that wasn't what I wanted. I wanted him to tell me what to want. I wanted guidance, from him, from the librarian, even though at that time I had never had the experience of reading a book I didn't like.

The reason my choices were crucial was that I was allowed to take out only five books at a time. I always finished all the books the same day I got them, and then I had the rest of the week to get through, absorbed in the highly unsatisfactory task of rereading. Why would I want to reread a book? I was interested only in books that would tell me something I didn't know.

I don't know what I read on those dry days. Nor do I remember any of the books I took out of the library. Except one. It was called *Minty's Magic Garden*. It was about a girl called Araminta. She had a garden full of magical plants. She wished for a brother and slept with a few sprigs of baby's breath under her pillow. Quite soon, the brother she desired was born.

The only reason I remember *Minty's Magic Garden* is that it

123

was one of the few things that traveled with me when we moved from our apartment to my grandmother's house after my father died. I hoped no one would find it. It was a souvenir, a talisman, a proof of a life lived with him that I was already beginning to doubt. But I knew I couldn't keep the book. It didn't belong to me. It belonged to the library.

My mother told the librarian the story of my father's death, explaining the lateness of returning the book. She would never, she wanted to make the librarian understand, have allowed this to happen in ordinary circumstances. She'd never had an overdue book in her life. The librarian waived the fee.

So I had to suffer doubly. Once, as a careless person, a delinquent, and again, as an object of pity. Three times, because I also suffered the loss of the book. But if I'd kept it, I would have been guilty of two sins: lying and theft. Loss, I knew, was preferable to that.

My father taught me to read very early. I was only three. So I have no memory of a nonreading self, no memory of print being an obstacle, of black type on white pages being anything but a smooth canal down which he and I can sail, well embarked, contented, with all the time in the world.

When my father and I are reading, we lounge and sprawl. He is on his green chair and I am on the floor near his feet. Or we are on the rose-colored couch with its upholstered flowers, or sitting up together on my bed. We are in a place where the people we live among don't go. They aren't readers. *We* are almost nothing else.

Reading with my father, I am always safe and he is always handsome. Not someone I have to worry about or be ashamed of. Not someone with missing teeth or ripped trousers or shoes that are too big. Reading, we're removed from anything that can accuse or harm us. If there's anything in a book I don't like, he makes it go away. Because I'm scared when we read *Peter Pan*, he takes a scissors and cuts out every reference to Captain Hook. He reads to me from a book full of holes, full of spaces, spaces he fills in with something he invents, something that will bring me joy.

I am in love with books, but not the books that other children have. I don't like the Little Golden Books, available in every drugstore and most supermarkets, stories about animals or trains or characters other children (but not me, my father won't allow it) see on television. He brings me books from the city, books like no one else's. Books that tell me things I need to know about my future life. A French coloring book called *La Jour de Jeanne*. He writes the translations over the words I cannot understand: comprehensible English ink above the locked French print. From this I learn something quite exciting: There are other languages, other ways to live. Not only ours, which seems so difficult. Words can be unpacked to reveal meaning, therefore worlds, in ways I hadn't suspected.

And my father has the key. *Le Jour de Jeanne*. He translates the title for me: 'Jane's Day.' Jane has a day very different from mine. She wears *sabots* and a kerchief. I can't remember anything else about her except the energetic steps she took in her *sabots*. And the wonderful tilt of her nose (not like my father's and mine; our noses hook, point down, indicate not good cheer and forward-lookingness but heaviness, seriousness, perhaps inevitably, wrong choices made too late, things taken only because they are what's left).

I don't color in Jeanne's kerchief or her little dog, to say nothing of her marvelous clothing. I wouldn't dream of spoiling the ador-able openness of the black lines enclosing nothing. What is import-ant for me is that my father has unlocked the words under the outlined shapes. His voice, unlocking. His writing, opening up.

I remember the first book I read, because its form was unusual. In the center of the cardboard cover was an oval hole. I believe the succeeding pages were meant to fill in the hole with different faces wearing different hats signifying different jobs, but I can't remember how it worked.

But both my father and I knew no ordinary job was in my future. The book we both took seriously in this regard was called *The Nuns Who Hurried*. In the lower right-hand cover was the modest attribution 'By one of them.'

It wasn't really a book, it was a kind of pamphlet, a series of pages stapled together. But not a glossy, like most pamphlets in the pamphlet rack in church. Plain matte paper. Witty pen-and-ink drawings. From it, I learned to read words that were hard for me, but only for a little while: 'missionary,' 'catechetical.' But soon I was as at ease with those words as with the words of the lush *Grimm's Fairy-Tales* he brought home one day. Or the English edition of *A Child's Garden of Verses* with his inscription in the front. 'My darling Mary Catherine, you have asked me to write you love letters in other languages, so here they are.'

In German, French, Greek, and Latin my father was writing that he loved me. Now forty years later, my vanity, my sense of superiority over all living women, makes me pat my hair, stroke my cheeks, as if I've just been complimented on my beauty. Was there ever a little girl who was given anything like this? A girl who asked her father for love letters in different languages and got them?

This is the world of reading and writing into which my father leads me. But he doesn't stop there; he doesn't stop even with our love for each other. Books will also lead me to my salvation. He gives me *Six O'Clock Saints*, from which I learn, besides the story of Saint Nicholas reassembling some little boys who'd been dismembered and then pickled, that 'color' can be spelled with a *u*, 'colour,' a way I know to be superior. And he gives me Father Lascelles's *A First Prayerbook for Young Catholics*. It has a blue leatherette cover with letters stamped in gold, pages edged in gold, and, on the frontispiece, a lamb, his paws folded, his body run through with a cross that somehow does not cause him to shed blood.

13

Into Terra Nova:
A Crossing with Books

LAURA L. NAGY

My first week in college I met a boy named Jack. I say 'boy' because, in fact, we were only weeks removed from twelve years of 'Boys' and 'Girls' painted on the restroom doors at school, and I recall feeling more than a little startled, that first dizzying week, that the labels had miraculously and rather precipitously changed to 'Men' and 'Women.' I did not know what it felt like to be a 'woman'; I was young and green and scared and very, very confused by this brave new world.

But the university did make an attempt to help us with the transition. There was the inevitable 'orientation,' and then classes finally started, and by sheer happenstance I sat next to Jack in a chemistry lecture hall the size of Montana. We chatted before and after the class and walked across the campus together toward our dorms. When a caravan of buses hauled several hundred clueless eighteen-year-olds from the city out to a retreat that first weekend, I was pleased at continued serendipity: there was Jack, sitting on the bus I happened to board, and we chatted comfortably as we left Denver and climbed high into the Rocky Mountains. In that breathtaking setting the freshman class was to reflect upon the changes washing across our decks and also, I presume, 'bond.'

Jack and I sat around the huge bonfire that Friday night, cautiously sharing our ambitions and doubts and fears, and making plans to hike up a mountain together the following day. Another fellow, whose name I don't remember but whose significance I can never forget, was showing off for the crowd in a loud and grating manner – leaping across the fire, holding forth fortissimo like a wannabe stand-up comic, and otherwise rather desperately calling attention to himself. In the process, he was ruining for

me the peacefulness and intensity of an evening of quiet exploration under the incomprehensible array of stars that choose to
show themselves with such clarity at altitude.

I'd seen the kid in the dining hall and had noted this behavior
before and I was just plain irritated by it. After he'd executed
still another embarrassing *grand jeté* over the coals, I turned to
Jack in utter exasperation and blurted, 'I can't *stand* that guy.
He's a damned big-mouth Jew.'

The stricken expression on Jack's face is etched so deeply into
my psyche that I carry it with me even now, thirty years later.
He didn't say a word, but while I was pathetically naive and
utterly tactless, I wasn't stupid. I knew what I had done. 'You
mean you're . . . ,' I said, but it wasn't necessary. I'd pulled the
trigger, let go the bow-string, sprung closed the trap with its cruel
shredding teeth, and there was no calling my weapon of destruction back. I knew too quickly and completely that no apology was
adequate to undo what I'd said, and I was horrified, after the
fact, that I'd said it. I'd grown up in the Midwest, entrenched in
a solid pocket of WASPs whose values I couldn't help but absorb
as if through osmosis. I knew two Jewish kids in my massive,
four-thousand student high school, and Jack's golden hair and
Missouri upbringing didn't fit my feeble stereotype at all.

Needless to say, we didn't hike the mountain the next day.
Jack found a ride back to Denver on a different bus, and despite
my continued attempts to undo my terrible mistake, he moved
his seat in class and avoided eye contact when we passed in the
hallway. I was devastated, for I knew how much I had hurt him,
and I cursed myself for my thoughtlessness, for having a mind
closed tight, for blindly accepting attitudes I had never examined, not once.

I began to read – not just my textbooks but the *New York Times*,
Newsweek, books on Judaism, ethics, social psychology, philosophy.
I learned a great deal that semester, not just about my course
subjects but about who I was, or, more accurately, wasn't. Essays
and news reports on depredations in Vietnam began to draw
my attention more and more; in high school I had ignored the
body counts and the evening news footage of young men with
bloodied, anguished faces, baffled by what they were doing and
wondering why they were there. In my town the philosophy I
breathed in and thus made a part of myself was clearly 'Let's
bomb the hell out of those damned gooks and show them what

the good old U.S. of A. can really do.' That autumn of 1967 I started to question that attitude for the first time, and in the course of two or three months swung completely from a hawk to a dove. In fact, I began slowly to swing around on any number of issues and old beliefs, and books were my pivot point.

It wasn't that at eighteen I was devoid of facts. As a youngster I didn't read books, I inhaled them. When I was in fourth grade I begged for a note from my teacher to the 'Library Lady' who monthly parked the unwieldy bookmobile in our school drive-way; I desperately needed liberation from the children's section and yearned to browse the higher grades' shelves. While my peers were still reading *The Golden Book of Horse Stories*, I was actually struggling with *Gulliver's Travels* (I didn't get very far, but I was certain a pretty good story was lurking in there somewhere, and when my vocabulary caught up to my ambitions, I discovered how right my instincts were). I landed upon the Laura Ingalls Wilder books, read every one, and hungered for more. Through my namesake's tales of hardship and determination I realized that girls, too, could be brave, strong, and steadfast; she made me think I had been born in the wrong century. I read Paul Bunyan tales and slipped away to a wooded world of magic, humor, and wry ingenuity. I found the biography section and lighted there for months; I began to see what men and women of strength and courage had done with their lives – Davy Crockett, Eleanor Roosevelt, Sonja Henie, Helen Keller, stories miraculous and inspir-ing. The world they faced was so different from my 1950s 'Ozzie and Harriet' milieu, which defined – even circumscribed – what I wore, what 'America' meant, what I was allowed to become, and, yes, what I was supposed to think.

The teacher's note (thank you, Miss Slozat) also said I could take out *more* books than the other kids, so I would emerge from the bus-cum-library with stacks that I would devour far before the creaking vehicle's next visit. I began to set my alarm for 5.30 because that gave me an hour or so to read while our rambling old farmhouse was still silent. I would creep out from my bedroom, turn on a single light in the living room, and sit on the large floor register, warming my toes and rear end, lost in other worlds until it was time to get ready for school. On weekend mornings I tiptoed to the bookcase in the hall while the rest of my family slept, chose a volume of the *World Book Encyclopedia*, carried it back to bed, and happily worked my way through it, cover-to-cover; I

learned about the elevation of the Alps, Brazil's major exports,
the Chicago fire, the freshwater fishes (boldly colored illustrations there), right up to, yes, xylophones and zebras. Those times
with books were honey that sweetened a life of relative isolation; while we were not far removed from civilization, it was
still a farm, none of my schoolmates were within walking or biking
distance, and my brothers were otherwise occupied with two boys
of analogous ages who lived nearby. So I educated myself about
wondrous places that existed beyond our farm and my small
elementary school, and I began to wonder what it would be like
if . . . well, whatever I was reading at the time.

By high school I was carrying a paperback with me constantly,
just in case I found a few spare minutes during the day. I recall
my favorite English teacher passing me by in the cafeteria and
noticing my copy of *On the Beach* atop my textbooks. She began
a discussion of the book and seemed rather surprised that I was
reading it. I was equally puzzled by her reaction; we'd had those
atomic bomb drills in elementary school, after all – sitting on the
floor in the hallway, our heads down between our knees – and I
had earned my Cuban Missile Crisis badge in junior high. By
high school I knew from my reading what the new phrase 'nuclear
holocaust' meant, and I could doodle rather impressive mush-
room clouds in the margins of my notebooks as I wondered about
just what kind of mess humanity had gotten itself into. Luckily,
that English teacher – who's remained a lifelong friend and mentor
– kept talking to me about my books. Books had helped me make
a connection with her, one that let me feel less lonely in a sprawling
and rather intimidating school where my peers were more concerned with catching a smoke in the restroom than the grinding
tragedy of *Ethan Frome*.

In addition, my college prep English program also required
attendance at a monthly book discussion – like I needed any
impetus to read another book. I was touched by *A Separate Peace*,
depressed by *The Catcher in the Rye* (but went off and read *Franny
and Zooey* on my own just to see what this guy was about), blown
away by *The Great Gatsby*, then and now a technical tour de force.
We were encouraged to look at fiction in a new, and for me,
captivating way; I discovered the meaning behind the words and,
seeing that, never read in quite the same way again.

At one book group meeting my senior year I was appalled when
our discussion leader, a man who'd been my teacher the preced-

ing year and whom I liked and respected, foisted Freudian implications upon *The Turn of the Screw*. I argued vehemently; I couldn't
imagine that Henry James had meant *that*, and as I left the room
at the end of the meeting I rather pointedly dropped the book
into the wastebasket by the door. It banged against the metal
quite satisfactorily and I made my exit. But my mentor, also
involved in the reading program, came skittering down the hall
after me, waving the book over her head as she came. 'You can't
do that,' she called, and out of respect for her I stopped. 'You
have to learn to think about things in a different way. Maybe
you don't agree with Frank's interpretation, but you have to accept
it as one of many possibilities. There are *always* other possibilities.'

Other possibilities. I took the book from her and still have that
same copy, the spine broken and pages yellowed with age. She
was telling me, in a kind way, what I was to learn so soon and
so painfully with Jack. I had read plenty of books and knew plenty
about *things* – geography and history and architecture and art
and animals. But I knew very little about *people*. I was still trapped
in a belief system that excluded those other possibilities my teacher
had so kindly warned me to consider. Until Jack I was oblivious
to the reality of other cultures, other belief systems, other interpretations of history and events, and unaware that the old views
I had been fed in my small, conservative home town were not
the only ones, but, instead, were often dreadfully uninformed
and unenlightened. Seeing myself through Jack's eyes was a revelation that has changed my life, and after that disaster at the
campfire, I consciously worked to open my mind through many
late nights alone in the quiet stacks of the university library, accom-
panied only by the hum of the fluorescent lights, the silent, stolid
books, and my own caroming thoughts.

And so I began to learn more about other people, and in the
learning, began to break free from some of the prejudices I had
grown up with. But books helped me to go beyond even that.
Through them I discovered not just the world and the rich variety
of people inhabiting it, their fascinating and often puzzling ways
of behaving, the kaleidoscope of customs, traditions, and beliefs;
through books I discovered myself.

From my earliest school days I always felt different, an out-
sider somehow. I accommodated for it well; in high school I had
lots of friends and worked hard to tell the best jokes and be the
life of the party so I would feel accepted. I attributed the difference

I sensed to a unique mindset, an intelligence that in my youth seemed more a curse than a blessing. I was different, I told myself, because I saw through a different lens, and for many years, that explanation was enough. But the incident with Jack, I realized over time, was only the start of a sea change; I never suspected, as I worked through the guilt from that awful, unthinking bigotry, that I would myself face the same kind of hatred, a hatred so powerful that it could snare even the self in its net.

During high school I dated a sweet, caring, and unerringly kind boy named Bill. We were the two smartest kids in our class, we took many courses together, we shared the same extracurricular activities, and therefore our matchup was not only perfect but also inevitable. I tried to fall in love with Bill, I really did. I tried to get excited when he asked me to go to the movies, play putt-putt golf, participate in picnics and hikes, swim, play tennis. We did have fun together, and dating Bill was easy and undemanding. We were still living in a period when, although rumor had it that guys on the football team carried 'rubbers' in their wallets, there was no pressure on us to have sex, to do drugs, or to drink alcohol. Our idea of a good time was to get hamburgers at a small local hang-out, and we weren't even labeled 'nerds' for it because the word didn't exist yet. We were on the cusp, at the end of an era, and luckily for me, it allowed me to pass for 'normal.' I didn't have to justify not sleeping with Bill; he didn't even ask it of me, and so the relationship could be safe and on-going. Now and then I'd break up with him because something seemed amiss, a nagging doubt subtle as the onset of a toothache. I was having a hard time making myself care for him as deeply as my girlfriends seemed to care for their guys. Occasionally Bill and I would have an ugly scene when I'd tell him I thought we should see less of each other; I was being honest – it really seemed so pointless. Bill would be terribly hurt, go off in a huff, and date other girls for awhile, but we kept drifting back together and even went to the senior prom. Somewhere I have a photograph of us, a young, rather puzzled-looking girl masquerading as a woman in a long turquoise formal and elbow-length gloves, posed with a young, bespectacled man in white tux and red cummerbund. Bill and I were the picture of innocence, and I think now, with some regret, of the times I hurt him because I was so far beyond innocence; I was deeply buried in ignorance and complete denial.

I had heard snippets, snickers, tiny, almost inaudible references to people so reprehensible no one even talked about them, and I began to have haunting suspicions about why I couldn't seem to feel the 'right' way about Bill. I just didn't love him, I told myself, that was all. When I felt love, it would be different – that's what we were taught in all the Doris Day and – irony of ironies – Rock Hudson movies. But what if . . .? So I did what I had always done when I needed to know something: I went to the library. I searched mightily and frequently for information, some book, some article that might help me fight back the doubts about myself. I found nothing, not a word, not a shred, not a hint. In 1967 a public library in a small, conservative Ohio town wouldn't dirty its shelves with books about 'deviants,' for heaven's sake. So I suffered, alone, uninformed, unable to ask anyone and unable to turn to books, which until then had always helped me find the facts I needed.

The story repeated itself in college. While I was able to read plenty of books about being human, this other thing without a name was virtually unacknowledged. Books had always been a chart guiding me into new territory, but all I could find even in the university library were guidelines in the home economics section on how to be a good wife and mother and small mentions in the psychology section of 'abnormal' or 'deviant' sexual behavior. Now, *that* was pretty comforting; not only was I different – who wants to clean house and bake pies? – but I was very possibly abnormal, crazy, and/or perverted, a prospect that made me run even further from the truth, completely terrified.

So there were other Bills, other frustrating and demoralizing attempts to shove myself into the mold that had been shaped for me and that I didn't dare question. The values I grew up with claimed that blacks were inferior, Jews were grasping, and women's career options were confined to teaching, nursing, or being a secretary (being a 'wife' was no career at all). And the condemnation of 'queers' wasn't even spoken, but it was implied everywhere around me; no mention of the lifestyle, no information to help me understand, only hetero stereotypes about what I was supposed to feel and do and be like. In the dorm we were passing around a dog-eared copy of *Everything You Ever Wanted to Know About Sex But Were Afraid to Ask*, and though I read the sucker from cover to cover, I found nothing in there about *me*. *Fear of Flying* was no help, either; what I was seeing all around me was fraternity parties, obligatory coupling, *Love Story* and

Looking for Mr. Goodbar. I was outside the loop. I didn't exist anywhere I looked, and for once, it seemed that books had failed me.

The books I needed were not dead, but sleeping. During graduate school I befriended a fellow female student in my department, and slowly and tentatively I began to admit to myself only
in a whisper that I enjoyed spending time with her much more
than with the men I was seeing. In time our relationship grew,
but not without wrenching difficulties as our ingrained, 'socially
acceptable' gender roles collided violently with the reality of what
we were feeling. Again, we were still in the Midwest, not in New
York City or San Francisco where we could easily have found
others like ourselves as well as, unimaginably, bars, restaurants,
clubs, support groups, and even bookstores for gays and lesbians.

Luckily, in academe a new discipline, Women's Studies, was
gaining strength and credibility, and books began to surface that
slowly led me to see myself in different ways. I began to read,
still apprehensive but nonetheless impelled by a powerful sense
of other possibilities; I was finally ready to undertake the transition from hawk to dove, from internalized homophobia to self-
accepting, whole human being. *Our Bodies, Ourselves* was a good
start; I knew practically nothing about my body or its character,
and I began to realize that self-hatred was not only unnecessary
but also destructive. Soon it was *The Feminine Mystique*, which
my uninformed and prejudiced self had previously dismissed as
claptrap; *Toward a New Psychology of Women* let me look into my
own mind; *A Room of One's Own*, *Mrs. Dalloway*, *To the Lighthouse*
created a new consciousness of women's ways of perceiving and
feeling, and Virginia Woolf's biography gave me a sense that even
'deviants' could accomplish great and beautiful things. I began
to find, through my reading, that the albatross I had been carrying around was not a 'wrong' vision of the world or even – most
comforting discovery! – so very 'different.' *Meeting the Madwoman*,
The Creation of Feminist Consciousness, *The Madwoman in the Attic*,
Women's Ways of Knowing – these and many more gave me a sense
of identity as a being who had the freedom and power to think
and act and inquire and even challenge old, established ways.
There were, I was discovering, other possibilities, other ways to
be a woman and, moreover, to be whole.

Slowly and quietly the libraries and bookstores in my part of
the planet finally started to have sections on gay and lesbian
issues, and I began to emerge from a long and painful darkness.

Rubyfruit Jungle – not my style, but my God, a book about lesbian experience! *Invisible Lives* – yes, I had been invisible, especially to myself! *Alma Rose* – a sweet, endearing tale of two women falling in love, as we had! *Permanent Partners* – my relationship was legitimate, a marriage in every sense of the word, an inherent good, not the pitiful dregs doled out to a damaged outcast! *Coming Out* – other people, fine, decent, ordinary people, had stories so much like mine! *Surpassing the Love of Men, Out in All Directions, Chloe Plus Olivia* – I *hadn't* invented homosexuality, I wasn't on my own in this, there was a long history, a heritage I was part of. In those books were names I recognized, men and women who had contributed mightily to society and were respected for what they had done and who they were. Gay and lesbian histories; guidebooks to 'gay-friendly' businesses, hostelries, employers; books on relationships, legal issues, parenting, finances. Newsletters, journals, magazines, and chatrooms. My isolation was over. I was connected to a culture I had first feared, then rejected, then accepted, then slowly embraced.

The embers of that long-ago campfire, by whose light I looked into Jack's tortured face and saw reflected my own prejudice, have been cold for three decades. Like Jack, I have been victimized by uninformed and unthinking acceptance of stereotypes; usually the bias came from others, but until books rescued me, some of it came from myself. Ignorance enslaves the mind and makes of it a fertile breeding ground for hatred and bigotry. I know I can't change others' attitudes; I can only follow my heart and live what I perceive to be a decent, caring, and kindly life. For awhile I couldn't do that because I was too frightened, a fear based on perspectives woefully limited by lack of knowledge, insight, and generosity. But books intervened, and I think I can say with certainty that they have not just shaped but saved my life. At college, they became a way to expiate my sin against Jack and, as soon as I was aware enough to think about it, against any kind of difference. In my professional life, they were bricks in the road toward degrees, guides while I was a journalist, intellectual infants I helped through the birthing process when I worked in publishing. Books give me the pleasures and rewards of reaching students, opening *their* minds as I once had to open my own. Books allow me to relax, laugh, and feel. Books have guided me to caring, stimulating, and lasting friends.

But books have enriched my life in a far deeper sense. They

led me to my true self; they have shown me how to be fully and committedly human and humane. They continue to support my attempts to extend my mental and spiritual territory. If life is exploration, and I think it is, I have made the crossing into terra nova with books in my hand. I can't think of a more valuable, trustworthy, and inspiring guide.

14

Sine Qua Non

FRANCES H. BACHELDER

There is a unique connection between books and music. To an individual who feels deeply the effects of reading, the response engendered by a moving piece of literature becomes almost an unreachable internal reflex similar to the effects that some musical works can elicit. The psychic and emotional responses to a story about war heroes, for example, correspond to those created by martial music: each stirs up deep, inner feelings.

One day, curled up on the couch with a book in my hands, I thought about this relationship. Studying the title on the cover, I felt a certain excitement, that of great expectations. I was reminded of the time my sister took me to the opera *Carmen* at the Metropolitan Opera House in New York City. Seated there in that vast, beautiful hall, I experienced the thrill of anticipation as I studied the cover of the libretto while waiting for the overture to start and the curtain to rise. Keeping that recollection in mind, I opened my book to the introduction. The orchestral music began. I turned to chapter one. The curtain rose slowly, the words on the first page of my book blending with the music. Mallarmé expressed it this way: 'In reading, a lonely quiet concert is given to our minds; all our mental faculties will be present in this symphonic exaltation.'

The 'music' of literature has been playing for me for a long, long time. I can't recall the first time I felt a book, but I do remember being 'read to' and the many times my father told me stories about his boyhood. He always began with these words, 'When I lived up on the farm. . . .' What happened there must have been exciting, because every night I asked for another story. It was a pleasing, comfortable refrain, and I enjoyed the stories as one enjoys a favorite song.

There have been many such favorite songs. At an early age, I was given a book called a 'primer' and to this day I can see it in my mind's eye. The green cover was well worn, leading me to believe that other members of the family must have read it, also. As to what it contained, I can only guess. But again, in the back of my mind, I see words beginning with each letter of the alphabet along with pictures describing the words. I wish I had it now. What memories the book might evoke, as much a reflection of my childhood as the teddy bear that was left behind when our family moved.

My love for books grew as I did, with the musical accompaniment following me into my youth. Although I was never much of a history student, I was impressed with a book of historical events, which I have read many times. Though its pages are slightly brown with age, it has survived the years remarkably well. The title? *America First* (1920) by Lawton B. Evans: one hundred true stories about our country and its people. As the author states in his introduction, 'The look of gratification, [on children's faces] when told that "it actually happened", was most satisfying to me. . . . It is hoped that . . . this collection of stories, covering the entire range of American history, will stimulate . . . those young citizens.' It certainly stimulated me.

My fondness for books is not limited to the fact that I like to read. The American bibliophile, Alfred Edward Newton, once said, 'We cherish books even if unread; their mere presence exudes comfort, their ready access, reassurance.' One of the rooms in the house where I lived at one time had bookcases along a wall. Because I was young, I'm quite certain I would not have expressed my feelings, as Newton did, about the books' 'presence.' However, I do remember how pleasurable it was to sit there alone, reading each title and author, exploring the names as some children explore a forest or an attic brimming with treasures: *Moby-Dick* by Melville; *A Tale of Two Cities* by Dickens; *Silas Marner* by Eliot; *Kidnapped* by Stevenson; and many others besides the classics. Although not a word was spoken, I sensed that we were friends. Somehow they had contrived to make me aware of them, and I spent time getting to know who they were.

My almost filial connection to books did not end with my childhood. I vividly recall an incident in a bookstore where I had gone in search of information on architecture. I walked directly down the first aisle and there on the shelf in front of me was exactly what I wanted; it was almost as if the book had called out to me. Had this been an isolated incident, I would have thought little of it, but it happened two or three times. Could there be some sort of magnetism or sense of direction, which I'm sure other people have experienced, that drew me to the book? Ultimately, it does not matter how or why it happened, but I'm convinced that there is a level of communication (other than reading) between books and people. Is it even possible, for example, to feel lonely when browsing the stacks in a library? I don't think so.

For me, books have always had a certain feel and distinctive odor that are as vivid but ineffable as the feelings I get from music. And so I realized early in life that I had a taste for books. This was, I believe, at least in part because of my family's love of reading. My father liked detective stories, E. P. Oppenheim being one of his favorite authors. I'm not certain, but I always suspected that the books my mother enjoyed were those with a romantic flavor. Every night Aunt Katie, a former teacher, went into the 'front room' and settled down with a book in her hands. I remember my sister sitting by the window, reading. Her total absorption fascinated me: From the moment she opened a book, nothing disturbed her. I seldom 'lost' myself in a book, but that did not interfere with my reading pleasure. Perhaps the ticking of the clock, the slamming of the screen door, the ringing of the telephone, and voices in the background were musical accompaniment to the scenes playing out in my imagination as I turned from page to page.

Although certain books that I read as a child might not be considered influential by some, nevertheless they had a profound effect upon me. One such book was *Uncle Wiggily*, created in 1910 by Howard R. Garis. As his son, Roger, recalled in a later book about the Garis family (*My Father Was Uncle Wiggily*, 1966),

Uncle Wiggily was, of course, a distinct personality. . . . He was my father as he himself would have acknowledged; but my father within the deep recesses of his unconsciousness . . . , where everything was an exciting adventure, and although danger might lie in wait along the way, in the end everything came out all right.

This was the Uncle Wiggily he wrote about, and this was the child within the man, who never left him as long as he lived.

For fifty years Howard Garis entertained children and adults with the adventures of 'Uncle Wiggily' known originally as 'Bedtime Stories.' How could anyone forget Uncle Wiggily Longears' automobile with its turnip steering wheel, or Nurse Jane Fuzzy Wuzzy, his muskrat lady housekeeper, or the hollow stump bungalow?

Many years ago my husband, our two sons and I lived in Amherst, Massachusetts, where the Garis family also lived at the time. I recall that Roger and his wife, Mabel, brought their son, 'Buddy,' to my Sunday School class. I knew he was the grandson of the well-known author and was delighted to have him in my kindergarten group. I wish I had made an effort to meet Howard Garis, but at that time I was interested in *what* he wrote rather than *how* he did it. What an opportunity I missed! I could have talked with Uncle Wiggily and his creator 'in person.'

But books can chronicle adults' fantasies, too. On 25 May 1961, President Kennedy told Congress, 'I believe this nation should commit itself to achieving the goal, before the decade is out, of landing a man on the moon and returning him safely to earth.' Thus the nation was committed to a tremendous challenge, and although I didn't realize it at the time, this was to be the start of my collection of books on space travel, a few of which are: *We Seven, First on the Moon, Thirteen: The Flight that Failed,* and *The Voyages of Apollo.*

This was terra nova for my reading focus, and I continued to gather as much information as possible about space science to add to my long-established interest in music and literature. I now have a bookcase almost filled with books about the many flights into space, and the strains these titles elicit are bold and fortissimo. The first moon landing on 20 July 1969, will always be a highlight for me. As of this writing, robotic devices have landed on Mars, and some day it is highly probable that humans will again set foot on the lunar surface. It has been said that 'good literature has the power to create vicarious experience . . . through the eyes of knowledgeable authors.' I'll have to make room for another bookcase.

One book that guided me through a more earthbound, but nevertheless challenging, adventure is the *Common Sense Book of Baby and Child Care* by Dr. Benjamin M. Spock. It was my sextant, my compass, and my map throughout the journey of parenthood. Much of it I read before the children were born and I followed the book's precepts almost to the letter during their childhood.

Whenever a question arose about what to do, I looked it up in 'Dr. Spock.' There were times, though, when I should have used my own common sense and read between the lines, because, naturally, children have their own ideas. The paperback edition, stained and torn and sporting loose, dog-eared pages, attests to the fact that it gave frequent and loyal service. Our sons, now grown men of whom we are very proud, have their own families, and through them and their children we are reliving those days, and the refrain plays again in their lives.

Our older grandson, now nine, said to me one day, 'I just *love* bookstores!' He was three years old when his father first introduced him to a shop full of books. I watched him one time as he stood looking at the books in the same manner I had seen his father study the bright colors, the shapes, the pictures, and the words several decades before: It was a look of sheer wonder. When a child about his age walked by, he took a book from the shelf and handed it to her, as if to share a great discovery. I smiled when I read the title: *How to Win Friends and Influence People* by Dale Carnegie. Coincidence?

Apparently that reverence for books and their magic starts at an early age, for one of our favorite snapshots is of our granddaughter, who, at the age of eleven months, is sitting on the rug looking at a picture book. I wonder what was going through her mind.

Another time, our younger grandson, then age three, was walking back and forth from the kitchen to the living room, a bundle of motion and energy as only toddlers can be. Suddenly he noticed his sister sitting on the couch next to grandpa, who was reading to her. Whether from curiosity or magnetism we'll never know, but with blanket in hand and thumb in mouth, he began to include them in the itinerary of his travels, stopping by for a few seconds off and on to look at the book, then continuing his trip from room to room.

Of course the real Mecca for us bibliophiles is the library. I shall never forget my first visit to the Huntington Library, especially the reading room. The overpowering feeling I experienced upon entering was unexpected and I stood still for a minute to catch my breath. The room had a musty-sweet odor, the unmistakable essence of books and their covers. Except for an occasional cough and the scraping sound of a chair on the floor, it was quiet and peaceful. People were hunched over the desks, absorbed in their work. Books were stacked neatly on shelves – even on the balcony – and I was anxious to become part of the scene. At that moment, my taste for books became stronger than ever. In my imagination, I heard a rousing welcome; and as I walked around, stopping here and there to take a book from one of the shelves, the familiar music in my mind began. Once again I was in a concert hall. Although many years have passed since that first entrée into the special world of the Huntington, the memory and feeling are still vividly with me, and like Proust's madeleine, entering a reading room of any library in the country can elicit them, intense and full-blown, again.

Fifteen years ago, I was asked if I would be interested in proof-reading and editing manuscripts, a type of reading I had never done. I accepted the offer. Engaging books in this unique way has been, and still is, a source of pleasure, and has afforded me a gainful insight into the difficulties of research and writing. One day while reading a book entitled *On Being a Writer* (1989), which consists of interviews with thirty-one great authors, I discovered that James Michener might 'get as many as 150 to 200 books on a subject, browse through them, check things, etc.' Tom Robbins told his interviewer that he purchases books for research to be done at home. Erica Jong, when asked if she found the research difficult, replied, 'I love doing research. It was the best part of working on the book.'

When I started this essay, I thought my personal experiences and previously published manuscripts would enable me to proceed with little or no research. I was wrong. Slowly but surely, books piled up on my writing table and on the floor. All those books for one essay? No, an idea or two from each perhaps, but also I couldn't resist reading unrelated material. Reading is not a discrete activity, encapsulated and disconnected from itself and other experiences. It is, instead, an act that connects, that branches from one book to another to another like the strands of a thickly twisted vine. Each part is both its own entity and at the same time connected to the whole; the leaf furthest from the ground is never-theless a component integral to the entire organism. One book is never really separate from another, in our intellects or in our experience.

In similar fashion, I often take an album of piano music from the cabinet intending to play one or two songs. But one song leads to another and inevitably I play through the entire album;

there is something organic, something holistic in the relationship we establish with both books and music. In *Psychology of Music* (1967), Carl E. Seashore says that 'music is essentially a play upon feeling with feeling, . . . that mystic inner something which is spoken of as feeling. . . .' I like to think of this definition as applying to words also. In fact, Beethoven is said to have 'inspired a half dozen novels,' and the relationship between music and literature was recognized much earlier. Joseph Wechsberg writes in *Story of Music* (1968) that in 1570, a group of men 'got together to exchange ideas' about the literary–musical connection. They talked endlessly 'about the combination of dramatic poetry and music though they couldn't agree whether the words or the music were more important.'

Henry Purcell in his *Dedication of Dioclesian* (1690) explains it this way:

> Musick and Poetry have ever been acknowledg'd Sisters, which walking hand in hand, support each other; As Poetry is the harmony of Words, so Musick is that of Notes: . . . Both of them may excel apart, but sure they are most excellent when they are joyn'd, because nothing is then wanting to either of their Perfections: . . .

For me as for Purcell, music and literature cannot be separated. Thus, the musical connection enhances my feelings for literature. Studies have shown that music has a strong impact on people's emotions, although nobody seems to know why. The same applies to words when they are arranged in a certain way. I cannot imagine my life without music and books; they are sine qua non – indispensable.

15

The Performer and the Reader

MICHAEL ELLIS

Don't think that because you are a magician you
don't have to know anything else!
                T. Nelson Downs, King of Koins

I spent thirty-five years of my life in the theatre, most of that
time looking for work rather than actually working, a normal
condition in the theatre and one that allowed plenty of time for
reading. For eleven years, from 1954 through 1964, I was fortu-
nate enough to be the owner and operator of The Bucks County
Playhouse. Located in New Hope, Pennsylvania, on the banks of
the Delaware River, it was one of the most storied summer theatres
in the country. Since I was the one who chose the plays, I was
happily forced to read about three hundred scripts a year. That's
a good way to learn quickly the difference between good and
bad writing. (Not that good writing necessarily means that the
play will be a hit. But that's another story.)

Those were the dying ember years of the artistic fires lit by
the great creators of the Bucks County legend. Still in residence
and very active in the local community at that time were Oscar
Hammerstein, Pearl Buck, James Michener, S. J. Perelman, George
S. Kaufman, Moss Hart, his wife Kitty Carlisle, Paul Whiteman,
Budd Schulberg and many others: an all-star cast if ever there
was one.

Every week before the Wednesday matinee I held a 'tutorial'
session for the apprentices, about fifteen of them, who, after all,
were paying their own expenses for the summer in order to learn
something about the theatre. Noon was lecture time and we were
all privileged that one of those wonderful writers would agree

to come and talk to the apprentices each week and also answer their questions. To this day my memory is seared by the sight of Moss Hart reeling out of the theatre and sighing, 'They haven't read anything!'

It is obviously not possible for an actor to find work if he cannot read, in the narrowest sense of that word. However, if his lines are the only thing he reads, he is short-changing himself, as Moss indicated. (Many television actors in small parts are concerned only about the number of lines they have since the pay scale increases if you have to learn more than a certain number.) However, the theatre has a great tradition that has nothing to do with the number of lines. There is a history of performance and of text of which every actor should be aware and even proud. If reading the plays and history that form part of that tradition doesn't make him a better actor, at least it offers the possibility of making him understand that he is part of that great tradition, one which does not yet exist in the world of television or even motion pictures, whose first thirty-five years were spent in silence. Of course, if you went to the movies in the early days, you had to be able to read because the titles on the screen told you what was happening. Today, all you have to do is listen, an entirely different process and a much lazier one.

The tradition of the theatre is much stronger in England, of course, much of it deriving from the powerful presence of Shakespeare and the apparently indelible memories of the great performers, running through the centuries from Burbage and Garrick to Olivier, Richardson, Gielgud, Guinness and a whole new crop who stand by, ready to replace them even as we watch. There was almost no female tradition of performance before this century since actresses prior to these years were beyond the pale. But how strongly one was created and carried forward by Edith Evans, Peggy Ashcroft, Wendy Hiller, Sybil Thorndike and Gladys Cooper and how gloriously it is being carried on today by a brilliant group of stage actresses which includes Maggie Smith, Judy Dench, Eileen Atkins and Vanessa Redgrave. Alas, in the United States I do not see on the horizon anyone to replace the Lunts, Fredric March, Maurice Evans, Rex Harrison, Leslie Howard, Katharine Cornell, Jane Cowl, Ina Claire, Helen Hayes, Eva Le Gallienne and other stars of the first half of the century. I know they are out there, just beyond the horizon, but they have yet to emerge from the shadows of off-Broadway and the regional theatres. Only Julie Harris, Jason Robards and Christopher Plummer come to mind as true stars and stalwarts of the living theatre. It's tough to make a living on the stage at any time but even more so today because of the few plays being produced. Our best dramatic performers have little choice: they turn to television and the movies. Because they make so much money in those fields it's also more difficult to get actors to commit to a play for a long run. In 1949 Louis Calhern signed a contract to appear on Broadway in *The Play's the Thing*. In that contract Mr. Calhern stipulated that he would 'play the play wherever it played as long as it played.' That doesn't happen anymore.

In the days of the great matinee idols, male and female, all discussions of the theatre revolved around their performances and the plays in which they were appearing. Today, alas, there are not many plays for the future greats to act in because the theatre has become dominated by musicals. If you consider the huge number of revivals on Broadway every year, you will realize how heavily the theatre must lean on its past. Our regional theatres depend almost entirely on revivals. All the more reason to read and read if you want to act. The plays are out there and you must read them. You must! Find them and read them. You'll get more jobs and be better prepared for them.

When I was in college in the late thirties, I read four or five plays every week without fail and with great pleasure. In those days more than 200 plays were produced on Broadway annually. Think of that! Sometimes there were as many as five shows opening on the same night. Obviously they were not all great plays but they were all reviewed by the critics of nine daily newspapers the following morning, not by only three, as happens in New York today. I felt that the more I knew about those plays the better equipped I'd be to deal with my dreamed-of future as a star. Not only were there plays to read but there were books of dramatic criticism from which to gain many different points of view. Publishers gathered the reviews of William Winter, George Bernard Shaw, George Jean Nathan, Brooks Atkinson, Walter Kerr and other critics and actually issued them in book form. It may be that someone has published a book of reviews written by a present-day critic, possibly *The Contrary Opinions of John Simon*, but so far no one, to my knowledge, has issued a volume of the work of the best drama critic writing in America today, John Lahr. All of this makes it more difficult for the performer to find something to read that will enhance his value to the theatre as well as to himself. Yet it's out there waiting for him, even crying out for him. Go and find it! Meanwhile, people who are not performers are doing the reading instead: stage directors, managing directors, artistic directors, producers, even backers. Help them!

After college I spent three and a half decades working in the theatre. It turned out that the reading hadn't made me a better actor, or possibly even a good one, but it did broaden my understanding of the theatre so that when I realized that I wasn't going to be a star after all, a decisive moment in my life, I survived nicely as a stage manager, producer, lecturer and occasional writer about matters theatrical. I tried to maintain the historical and performing traditions of the theatre from the other side of the footlights. It's extremely difficult to do that today because to most people theatre today is a musical theatre. Few new plays are published these days and few performers read plays anymore. Most of them play their CDs of hit musicals instead. Present company excepted, of course.

Still, a young actor named Diedrich Bader sums up my case best, surely without his realizing it. A recent graduate of the North Carolina School of the Performing Arts, the first such school in the country, Bader was lucky enough, or talented enough, to land a job on the Drew Carey television show, which turned out to be a hit. 'It's just farce,' he says, 'the same old structure. I use bits that Molière wrote and people think they're great. I say, 'Well, I *read*.'' (Emphasis his.) Most television and motion picture performers do not. Pity! Most stage actors do. I hope!

When I think of the performing arts, I tend to think first of the theatre, then of motion pictures, followed by television. However, someone with a different background might well think of singing or dancing first of all. Others might give precedence to classical musicians, mimes, readers of poetry, rock artists, anchor men and women, talk show hosts, public speakers, magicians or even athletes. (Surely the best second baseman in the world is as thrilling to watch as the best dancer.) All of these artists are performers, whether in a small room for ten people, in a stadium or amphitheatre for one hundred thousand spectators or on a screen seen around the world by millions.

Of all these arts, and there is surely art in all of them, classical musicians and magicians are most deeply beholden to tradition, closely followed by golf. I have never met a classical musician who has not read deeply in the lives of the composers and studied the variety of interpretations, over the years and even the centuries, of any particular piece of music. It would be unthinkable for him to play any of the great classics without complete knowledge of the composer and his work. That is one of the reasons it is so difficult for new works to obtain a hearing. Neither orchestra nor audience knows anything about it and is therefore not comfortable with the idea of it. It takes time for something to become a tradition and more time in the world of classical music than in any other. It has taken roughly one hundred years for Bruckner and Hindemith to become part of the tradition rather than be thought of as newcomers. (And Hindemith is probably still thought of that way.) That is not necessarily a bad thing since ultimately it makes for excellent performances of their work. Time, time! Early in this century Stravinsky was impossible to understand, let alone like and enjoy, unless you were truly a member of the avant-garde, or wanted people to think you were. Today he is completely accepted. In another fifty years or so we may have the answer on John Cage and Phillip Glass.

Most beholden to tradition in the performing arts are magicians, whose art goes back to the Bible, when rods were turned into snakes and bushes were burned, or were they? More books are written about magic in proportion to the number of people practicing the art than on any other subject except medicine. And more magicians read them than do the performers in any other art. It is not possible to find a magician, professional or amateur, who is not aware of his predecessors and their contribution to the art. While there are at most only about five hundred people in the United States who make a living solely from the practice of magic, all thirty thousand interested practitioners of the art know who Kellar, Thurston, Blackstone and Houdini were. Houdini died more than seventy years ago and is still the biggest name in magic. For the public he is usually the only name it knows in magic. Magicians for the most part are not known by name but by what they do, the particular trick or miracle or illusion. If you were to stop a hundred people on the street and ask them to name three magicians, ninety-nine per cent of them couldn't do it. If you were to stop a hundred people on the street and ask them the name of the magician they saw on television last night, only about fifty per cent of them could name him. How-

ever, every one of them would remember that they saw David
Copperfield flying through space last night and were thrilled
beyond words.

And yet magicians themselves read. Oh, how they read! Without that reading they could not learn how to saw a lady in half
or walk through a brick wall or suspend your disbelief. Order
any trick from a magic catalogue and you will find at the top of
the instructions a history of the various elements which go into
the trick and the names of the people responsible for the creation of those elements. I can think of no other art which is so
conscientious about giving credit where credit is due.

Many people would be aghast at the suggestion that sports or
athletic endeavors in general are performing arts but in my view
they assuredly are. Certainly no publicly displayed performing
skill is greater than that of the previously mentioned second
baseman, whoever he may be, or Michael Jordan on a basketball
court, Tiger Woods at his best or any professional skier or figure
skater. I do not really know whether athletes read but for most
of them it certainly seems not to be a high priority. (It is said
that Ted Williams refused to read anything because he used his
eyesight only to watch a baseball coming at him at ninety miles
an hour and was unwilling to risk switching his sight from distant
viewing to close-up.) In 1997 the fiftieth anniversary of Jackie
Robinson's breaking of the color barrier in the major leagues was
celebrated and it was discovered that there are baseball players
who had never heard of him. A pitcher who broke a long-standing
record held by Whitey Ford had never heard of the man. The
main reason for this is that many players in the major leagues
today are familiar with the game but not with its history in this
country because they come from other countries where the game
is what counts, not the history of it. In discussing reading we
tend to think of it as reading in English but as the world becomes multi-cultural we have Russians in the National Hockey
League, Japanese and Latinos in the baseball majors, Scandinavians
and middle Europeans in the National Basketball Association and
professional tennis players from more than thirty different countries. All of them add color and quality to their sport. However,
think of this: many of them have interpreters at their side during
all their working hours so that they may communicate with their
teammates. Imagine having to read in a language you don't even
speak.

In the United States, and to an even greater extent in Great Britain, golf is the greatest keeper of the flame of tradition. Every golfer of any stature knows who the great golfers were, what they achieved and where they achieved it. The most literary of sports writing is about golf, although sports writers in general are very good indeed. But golf is in a class by itself, partly because of the character of the game and the pristine sportsmanship of its players in an era when sportsmanship has almost disappeared and partly because of the traditions it so fiercely clings to.

And yet, and yet. We live in an age when there are those who feel that reading isn't really necessary, that it is slowly disappearing anyway. We now have video tapes, computers, discs of all kinds, talking books. Learn golf while watching Greg Norman on a tape. Learn magic from watching teaching tapes by the greatest living magicians. Listen as our greatest actor reads our greatest novel while you speed along the superhighway and thrill to it. Well, maybe.

I don't listen to books on tape because the reader does not go at my pace. He goes at his pace. I want to go at my pace. I also want to turn back a page or skip a page when I feel like it. The tape plows right ahead and doesn't know that. I think it is possible to learn a magic trick from a tape, but not without a book at hand. As you watch the tape, you run the risk of trying to be the magician who is teaching the trick and you aren't that magician. You're you, the only such you in the world. The tape also cannot answer your questions, even though it may try to anticipate them. You may have to start and stop that tape a hundred times to pick up the subtleties of what the artist is doing. So, by all means have a book of instructions in hand. Read them and profit from them, using the tape as a supplementary tool.

T. Nelson Downs said, 'Don't think that because you are a magician you don't have to know anything else!' That of course applies to anyone who professes to be a performing artist. It's simply gospel. Be an actor, a singer, a dancer, a magician, a golfer, what have you. But first of all be a human being, an estate more easily reached by reading, reading, reading. Then apply that reading to the experience of living and you'll be a better actor, singer, dancer, magician, golfer or what have you. Easy, isn't it?

In the end it all comes down to a very simple proposition: Reading is better than not reading, just as breathing is better than not breathing.

Part Three
Future Concerns

16

Literature without Books?

LAURENCE LERNER

I begin with a few incidents which show how much books have meant to people.

1. 'A' is looking round a junk shop in the provincial town he sometimes visits. Among the dusty pile of books he finds an eighteenth-century scientific treatise, with the back cover missing. Idly wondering if these outmoded explanations of optics are worth even 50 pence, he notices that it is abundantly annotated in an ink now faded to dull brown. On an impulse he buys it, and after deciphering the annotations, studying dates, and spending a few days exploring biographies and bibliographies, he decides that they are by Coleridge. With mounting excitement, he writes to all the Coleridge scholars he can think of.

2. 'B' was a soldier in the First World War. In the hell of trench warfare he carried a pocket Milton with him. As the shells whined overhead and the machine guns rattled, he read how Death 'snuffed the smell of mortal change on earth'. The book accumulated mudstains and bloodstains; one page was torn out, so he was never sure what happened 'from the North of Norumbega and the Samoed shore', nor, since he had no reference books with him, where Norumbega and the Samoed shore were. If there was enough light, he would read himself to sleep with 'Tower'd cities please us then/ And the busy hum of men'. Almost every line took on a resonance from dangers it had lived through with him; when the war was over, the book was his most treasured possession. He found he didn't want to possess a bigger, cleaner, properly annotated edition of Milton; as the horror of the trenches began to fade, he more and more thought of them as the place

where eldest Night
And Chaos, Ancestor of Nature, hold
Eternal Anarchy, amidst the noise
Of endless wars . . .

3. From 'Detached Thoughts on Books & Reading' by Charles Lamb: 'Thomson's *Seasons* . . . looks best (I maintain it) a little torn, and dogs-eared. How beautiful to a genuine lover of reading are the sullied leaves, and worn-out appearance, nay, the very odour (beyond Russia) if we would not forget kind feelings in fastidiousness, of an old 'Circulating Library' *Tom Jones* or *Vicar of Wakefield*! How they speak of the thousand thumbs that have turned over their pages with delight – of the lone sempstress, whom they may have cheered (milliner, or hard-working mantua-maker) after her long day's needle-toil, running far into midnight, when she has snatched an hour, ill-spared from sleep, to steep her cares, as in some Lethean cup, in spelling out their enchanting contents! Who would have them a whit less soiled? What better condition would we desire to see them in?'

4. 'C' was a political prisoner. He spent much of his time in solitary confinement: his companions were bedbugs, snatches of sound from the corridor, shouts of protest or solidarity from other cells, and his own thoughts. He tried to think systematically, but memory would tease and elude. He begged the warders to bring him books, and one day three books were brought: he was never sure if it was a special concession, or an unofficial act by a kindly warder. One was in a language he couldn't read; the second was a volume of speeches by the president of the country that had imprisoned him; and the third was the *Autobiography* of John Stuart Mill. He struggled to learn some grammar from the first, with very limited success; he made up obscene parodies of the second – and these occupations filled many of the endless hours. Easily the most valuable was the Mill, which he read again and again, and thought about when not reading it, till he knew whole paragraphs by heart. Sometimes he bitterly envied the stability of Victorian England, where arbitrary imprisonment was unknown; sometimes he told himself that arbitrary imprisonment is the norm, everywhere – what changes is the choice of victim and the excuses that are given. Sometimes he envied the certainties in Mill's life, the solidity of his achievement; at other times he felt that Mill had never recovered from his breakdown, and thought the chapter

title 'A Crisis in My Mental History' should be the title of the whole book. When eventually he was released, he told himself it was this book that kept him sane.

5. Edgar, a young dropout in Berlin in the days of the GDR, is living (without police permission) in a summer house, trying to invent a new paint-sprayer for the factory from which he got the sack. Sitting on the lavatory he finds there is no paper except a tattered cheap edition of an old book. He has used up the title page before he thinks of reading the book, so he never finds out who it's by or what it's called. He is never sure whether the book is pompous rubbish or strangely important, but he reads it over and over, quotes it to everyone, and sends bits of it on tape to his friend Willi, who thinks it's a code. He never finds out that the book is Goethe's *Werther*, but German readers (along with the theatre audience when it was dramatized) realize instantly that *Die neue Leiden des jungen W.*, by Ulrich Plenzdorf, is a rewriting of the Werther story, an example of what Genette would classify as 'transposition' (the most important of the various kinds of 'hypertextuality'): Edgar W. is re-enacting, without knowing it, the story that took Europe by storm in the 1770s. The tattered old paperback in the lavatory is the ironic chorus to an otherwise commonplace story about a young rebel against respectability.

6. In 1909 Arnold Bennett published a book called *Literary Taste*, in which he declared 'Literature is first and last a means of life, and the enterprise of forming one's literary taste is an enterprise of learning how best to use this means of life. People who don't want to live, people who would sooner hibernate than feel intensely, will be wise to eschew literature.' This idealistic aim was followed by a piece of very down-to-earth advice: 'surround yourself with books, create for yourself a bookish atmosphere.' 'Theoretically,' he declared, 'an amateur of literature might develop his taste by expending sixpence a week, or a penny a day, in one sixpenny edition after another sixpenny edition of a classic, and he might store his library in a hat-box or a biscuit-tin. But in practice you would have to be a monster of resolution to succeed in such conditions. The eye must be flattered; the hand must be flattered; the sense of owning must be flattered.'

7. Then there are the beautiful books, beautifully printed and beautifully bound, by the Peter Pauper Press or the Folio Society or even more expensive publishers. I have a few in front of me as I write: Lord Chesterfield's letters to his son, with a black spine

and exquisitely marbled covers in red, white and black; Frances Trollope's *Domestic Manners of the Americans*, with a nicely drawn map on the end-papers and contemporary lithographs, quaint, comic and vivid, by one August Hervien; *The Trial and Execution of Socrates* with a fine scarlet cover and drawings by my favourite among recent British artists, Michael Ayrton, which succeed in making Socrates at once ugly and fascinating.

8. And finally the old books, those that belong, as physical objects, to the past that so many reprints emerge from. I have a large folio *Shakespeare Memorial* published in 1864 for the tercentenary. It prints many of the documents that Shakespeare scholars use, such as the Preface and Commendatory Verses to the first Folio, along with extracts from Stratford Corporation accounts in the sixteenth century, and discussions of Shakespeare's characters, which tell us that the atmosphere of *Romeo & Juliet* 'is quite unEnglish', and that King Lear 'is a Celt and displays the characteristics of his race'. The illustration of Shakespeare and Ben Jonson arguing at the Mermaid Tavern stands opposite one of a huge black-bearded (and quite unNegroid) Othello glowering sternly at Desdemona pleading 'I hope my honoured lord esteems me honest'. Paging through it I become a mid-Victorian, seeing Shakespeare through the eyes of my great-great-grandfather.

There we have some variations on the age-old theme of celebrating books: some are taken from my own experience, some are quoted, some are freely adapted from sources I have read and remembered (or misremembered). They seem to me very similar to what a hundred other authors and book-lovers have written.

But this is 1998, and we are in the electronic age. Books, we are told, sometimes with delight, sometimes with sadness, are nearing the end of their life. In the future, instead of browsing lovingly through a volume, we shall surf the internet; instead of cutting pages we shall log in; instead of sitting back in our armchair holding the volume we shall sit up at our desk watching the screen or even (I have been told) stay in the armchair and cause the text to appear in the air in front of us. We shall dismantle our bookcases, turn them into shoeracks or shelves for ornaments. There will be no need to complain (that complaint that is always something of a boast as well) that we have no more room in the house for books, since the whole of *War and Peace* now fits easily onto a single disc. Already television presenters like to say 'I don't read books much – does anyone any more?' as they introduce programmes about Greek mythology or hunting for a lost novel by Kipling. If you haven't actually read any Kipling, you can tune in to those who have, who will obligingly read you a few key paragraphs. Hunting for a lost work is, no doubt, an odd experience for someone who never reads: to him all books are lost.

The great beneficiary of electronic systems is certainly scholarship. To write our critical articles on (say) sex, motherhood and gender relations in nineteenth-century poetry, we shall no longer need to rely on memory, or waste time reading anything unnecessary, since the *Cornell Index to English Poetry* will find for us all the poems that contain the words *love*, *breast*, *baby* and *masterful*. And if you want to study how the poem came into being, you will be able to consult an electronic variorum of Wordsworth or Shelley: you will be able to call up on your screen every version from the first draft to the final rewriting, instructing your program, if you wish, to highlight the words that remained unchanged or the words that only appeared at the nth revision. Here is an insight into how Shelley wrote which Shelley himself might not have been able to give you. Here, when the scholar-programmer has done his work, is the key to the process of writing, poised to pluck out the heart of the mystery.

I spoke once to one of the editors of the new electronic edition of Shelley. Dazzled and awed by his account of the wonders of technology, and what the reader of the future would be able to learn about the poems, I could think of only one criticism. 'This will be wonderful for the Shelley scholars,' I said, 'but what of the person who just wants to read Shelley's poems? Will your edition be any use to him?' 'Well,' said my interlocutor, 'we clearly use words in a different sense. To me, what I'm offering *is* reading.'

Let us now go through these eight bookish experiences I began with, and ask if they are outmoded. Do they belong only to the past? If books cease to exist, how much will be lost? Does the death of the book mean the death of literature?

First, the marginal annotations. The Coleridge of the future who is no longer able to use a pen will still be able to annotate the books (or should we now say 'texts'?) that he reads. He is sure to have a program in his word-processor that enables him to add comments to the text, in a different font or a different colour when printed out, and he will be able to put in cross-references to his heart's content. But what of the book-buyer, what of 'A' picking up his lucky bargain? The annotations may never leave the machine. If they *are* printed, they would seem to belong more to Coleridge's notebooks or papers than his library, and they will never, surely, appear on a second-hand stall. Scholarship, wedded to thoroughness, may have to do without its occasional extra-marital affairs with serendipity.

Second, Edgar and the tattered paperback. I can imagine Plenzdorf (or someone) writing a story about a young man surfing the internet and coming across a classic text which he does not recognize; young Edgar – bright, rebellious, half-educated, technically skilful, is just the sort of hero for such a story. I can even imagine it being turned into a play, with a gigantic screen projected above the character's head, but it would be, surely, a very static play. And it would certainly lose its teasing hint of the improper – the highly unliterary use to which the book has been put!

Our political prisoner may well have profited from the fact that books, precious at some times and to some people, are also seen at times as mere rubbish. If he was given his books because a kindly warder found them on a junk heap and thought he might as well pass them on to the unoffending bloke in cell 74, then this casual act transformed dross into gold. Of course the warder might find some discarded disks, but the prisoner would not, surely, have had a computer in his cell, let alone a computer programmed to read just those files. Books need no technology to be read – a blessing to those who lack it.

Next, the pocket Milton in the trenches. We can hope that the 'B' of the future will not have to fight in a war; if, unhappily, he does, it will surely not be a war in the trenches. But unless he is posted to the operations room he will surely find it much more convenient to carry his Milton as a book than as a disk. True, computers are getting smaller, and he might be able to carry one in his pocket, but making sure of an electricity supply or a functioning battery will never, surely, be as easy as opening a volume.

Or as pleasurable. Neither a future Bennett nor the purchaser of Folio Society volumes is going to enjoy switching on and logging in as he enjoys looking along the shelves, stroking the leather binding, or coming upon the illustrations. The reason for this is

obvious: the physical existence of a book is more important than
the physical existence of an electronic file. Who derives sensu-
ous pleasure from the pale grey of his computer casing, or the
electron flow across the screen?

But literature is already one remove from physical existence in
a way that distinguishes it from the other arts. The painting belongs
on the canvas, the sonata emanates from the piano, architecture
is a set of buildings: we cannot in the same way claim that the
'Ode to the West Wind' is any particular printing of it. Words
are the only signs that we can with confidence divide into signifier
and signified. True, a painting can have a symbolic meaning, and
a crucifixion can in a certain sense be the signifier of the Atone-
ment or the Redemption, but in a far looser and more disput-
able sense; and in the case of music any attempt to claim that a
sonata 'signifies' something stateable in words would relegate it
to the category of programme music. To confirm the view that
literature is not connected to its physical embodiment as a painting is connected to the canvas and the pigments, we have only
to think of learning a poem by heart. This does not reduce it, or
deprive it of its true existence – many would claim that it brings
us closer to the poem itself. A poem on a disk, called up on a
screen, is in one way like a poem learnt by heart: it no longer
needs the book.

So we must concede that the loss suffered by a literary work
when it is no longer in book form is not, in the strict sense, a
literary loss. Whereas pigment and canvas are essential to the
painter, books are a convenience to the writer – so great a convenience that it took the invention of computers to show us that
they are not essential. (Or to remind us: for there was, of course,
literature before there was printing.)

So are we to conclude that, though literature will continue,
books will be superseded? And that it would be no great loss if
they were?

The answer to the first question is, Who knows? For none of
us can see so far into the future; but my answer to the second is
a strong No, for a reason that has not yet been mentioned. We
do not live in a world of stark alternatives and pure essences. It
is intellectually valuable, I believe, to explore the distinctions I
have been trying to draw, to ask what is essential to the experience of literature and what is extraneous, but that does not mean
we are condemned to a kind of conceptual puritanism that has

to live without the extraneous. The financial wizardry of the Chancellor of the Exchequer is not the reason you voted his party into office; your wife's dark eyes and earning capacity are not the reasons you married her; the optional extras offered by the tour guide are not the reason you chose that holiday; but this does not mean you must not feed deep upon her peerless eyes, or not go on the optional outing, or insist that a nonentity run the country's finances. And the pleasure of casting your eye along the bindings, the feel of turning the pages, the fascination of second-hand bookshops, the dog-eared copy of *Werther* turning up in the lavatory, the sullied leaves and worn-out appearance of Lamb's copy of *The Seasons* – none of these is, in the strict sense, a literary experience. But – strict sense? Who wants to live in a world where sense is always strict?

17

The Sad Demise of the Personal Library

JAMES SHAPIRO

I rescued the core of what was to become my scholarly library from a garbage truck in New York City in the spring of my senior year at Columbia. Early in the morning on my way to a part-time job, I spotted some sanitation workers dumping boxes of books into the back of their truck. I picked up a couple of volumes that had spilled onto the ground. I couldn't believe my good fortune and asked them to stop. They were amused and helped me retrieve perhaps 60 or so books from the hopper – mostly literary criticism and Shakespeare scholarship. No doubt some disgruntled graduate student had called it quits and dumped the lot. This serendipitous encounter came at a critical time for me and helped tip the balance in favor of my deciding to get a Ph.D. in English (happily, I chose not to interpret it as a dire warning about my choice of careers).

Expanding that fledging library became one of my preoccupations during my years in graduate school at the University of Chicago, where friends and I would pile into a car to make the rounds of local secondhand bookshops. There was little chance of our equaling the collections we saw in the offices of professors such as John Wallace, who had been able to buy cheaply in postwar Britain first editions of most of the major works of the English Renaissance, or Michael Murrin, whose office was crammed floor-to-ceiling with books we had never even heard of.

Still, we could afford to buy hardcover books for a few bucks – important out-of-print books, which were set out every Friday morning at 11 at O'Gara's Bookshop. Down the block, at the Seminary Co-op, we could find the best recent scholarship if we could manage to shoulder our way through the crowd surrounding the table holding new arrivals. Long before we discovered Walter Benjamin's brilliant essay on 'Unpacking My Library,' we had come to understand that an essential part of the culture of graduate school, unspoken because it was so clearly understood, was creating a personal library.

A couple of decades later, I'm not so sure that the same value is still placed on building a library. Recently, a story ran in *The New York Times* about scholars whose personal libraries were so immense that their apartments contained little else. A few days later, someone wrote to the newspaper noting that what was left unmentioned in the story was that all these overflowing libraries belonged to people 'of a certain age.' He compared them with younger American scholars who lived in apartments with 'clean, virtually empty bookcases.' The letter dovetailed with my own impression that – with some striking exceptions – few graduate students, and even fewer undergraduates, in American universities are actively encouraged these days to buy books and build their libraries.

Curious as to whether professors were buying as many books as they used to, I asked sales directors at several university presses about trends over the past decade or so. They all said the same thing: Except for scientists (whose purchases are often covered by grants), scholars are not buying as many books as they once did – even while many of them complain about the death of the monograph or the difficulties of getting published.

Press directors also report lukewarm response among scholars to publishers' mail-order catalogues. The directors say that these catalogues generate less of a return each year, even as they become more expensive to produce. The same holds true for sales of books at professional meetings. I was told that even when scholars buy books at these meetings, increasing numbers wait for the last day to make their purchases, when many books are reduced to half-price. And, increasingly, the books they do buy tend to be in paperback. Since a book's break-even point has traditionally depended upon a balance between hardcover and paperback sales, this shift in professional book-buying habits has put an additional financial strain on university presses.

Even as the paperback is fast replacing the hardcover book in the scholarly library, the course packet is displacing the paperback in the graduate and undergraduate classroom. Poised between the printed text and the internet, the current academic world is increasingly defined by the course packet. I have witnessed a shift in my own department in the past decade from syllabi that are driven by books – almost always paperbacks – to those that are based on photocopied readings. Where once these packets contained only supplementary readings, many of them – in thick binders – now contain the readings for the entire course.

I'm not sure why they have become quite so popular. I recognize the appeal of course packets, especially in emerging fields where it's often impossible to find materials in book form. Issues of convenience and cost no doubt also figure in. No less troubling than issues of potential copyright violation, however, is the message that course packets quietly underscore: Reading material is ultimately disposable. Students buy a course packet, share it with friends (who perhaps photocopy the photocopy to save a few dollars), and, when the course is over, toss it out. The long-term cost to publishers and to authors who depend upon the next generation of scholars to buy serious books is incalculable. If, in the coming years, graduate students who have come of age in the culture of the course packet rely on photocopied materials in assignments to their own classes, what is the likelihood that university presses will be able to afford to publish their scholarship?

Another reason for the decline of book sales to academics, especially young ones, is that it's not just books that are temporary and disposable, but the scholars who once bought them. With many graduate students entering their profession as adjuncts or on short-term contracts, and with many faculty salaries barely keeping pace with the rising cost of living, it's not surprising that fewer academic books are being purchased. And since adjuncts don't get permanent office space, many instructors do not have a place to store books, a place from which to lend a volume to a colleague or a student, a place in which a student during office hours can see a teacher surrounded by books.

I'm one of the lucky ones: I have an office and my books have a permanent home there, though this too brings with it some unexpected consequences. A decade ago, my office was broken into – the lock carefully picked by a professional thief. Gone were my best books: editions of Elizabethan plays and poems, works of criticism that were long out of print, books that had been given to me by retiring mentors and colleagues.

It turns out that the thief had been working the campus regularly: I was told that he had also devastated the collections of a couple of art historians. A few weeks later, I got a call from a friend and fellow book buyer who had spotted my books down-town at the Academy Bookstore. Though I explained to the book-seller that the books were stolen, in the end I had to buy them back at two dollars each. Had I gone to the police, they would have impounded the books as evidence for who knows how long. At the time, I was furious; these days, I catch myself longing for a time when there were thieves who were as adept at picking books as they were at picking locks.

Nostalgia has probably always gone hand in hand with book collecting. It may simply be habit by now, but I cannot imagine teaching or writing without having my books at hand. For some reason, it has always been the ideas that come to me at 3 in the morning – ideas that never seem to survive intact until the univer-sity library opens – that have mattered most to my teaching and scholarship. At those moments, it is a great comfort to search my shelves and find the book that will make the crucial connection.

When Walter Benjamin wrote of his library earlier in this century, he was conscious of living at a time when the scholarly library was in decline; it's hard to imagine what he would make of our current situation. It may well be that in a few decades, the personal electronic library (surely an oxymoron) largely will have replaced the kind of libraries to which intellectuals have turned for a couple of thousand years. If that ever happens, a good deal will be lost – a sense of community and continuity, of books changing hands from generation to generation, of the fellowship of the book-buying expedition. Most of all, we will have lost serendipity – the acci-dental encounter with a book that changes your mind and maybe your life.

18

The Future of the Academic Book

GILL DAVIES

INTRODUCTION

When people talk about having 'A Passion for Books', more often than not they are implicitly referring to general books. If we are asked to name a book which has had a great influence on us – a book we could not do without – probably nine out of ten of us will cite a great novel. These books possess a spiritual dimension, quite rightly regarded as something to be preserved. In any discussion about books, however, we must not forget the legion of other books – specialist publications – that in many ways can be equally influential: namely, academic, educational, scientific, technical and medical.

Most specialist publishers do not regard themselves as being in the 'life enhancing' business but many – in all modesty – would like to believe that what they are publishing is something which does enhance knowledge and understanding in their chosen subject area, and still see the book has the main means of continuing that. Moreover, these books are often the place where new ground is broken, where new ideas and original research are presented, which will eventually filter down to popular consciousness and influence many areas of perception and endeavour. The question of the health and sustainability of the book is therefore as important for specialist publishers as it is for those who are publishing books for a general readership.

The relationship between specialist publishers and their market is inevitably a very close one. Unlike general readers, who buy their books for a variety of reasons amongst which the requirement of need is less likely to feature, specialist book buyers have needed the content of their book purchases for study, examination, writing and research. The specialist market is still overwhelmingly obtaining the knowledge and information it requires through the printed page, but the question, 'for how much longer?' is one that looms large in many specialist houses, including academic ones, whose books are the subject of this contribution.

While the fortunes of general publishers are thought to be subject to the whims of public taste and interests and their need to compete for leisure spending power, academic publishers are often seen as cushioned from market forces because their books come under the heading of 'must haves'. But academic publishers are highly dependent on 'the public purse', because their performance is so closely linked to the financial good health of the higher education sector. In recent years, the finances of this sector, in the United Kingdom anyway, have been rather volatile. In addition to this financial factor, we must add what is now seen as the greatest threat of all to the book – digital technology. In no other market has the coming of the digitization of text been greeted with as much enthusiasm as it has within the university sector.

A PASSION FOR DIGITAL TECHNOLOGY

There are two main reasons for this. The first is that electronic networks that allowed people to communicate with each other through a computer and a modem, and therefore enabled text to be transmitted down the line, were primarily developed within the university sector. To begin with they were seen as a way of allowing academics to communicate with each other: as an easy means of sending their latest research papers, or comparing and contrasting research findings. As was often said, the solitariness of the desk, the chair and the computer screen, was ideally suited to the monk-like character of the academic, absorbed in his or her subject. The academic market, therefore, is not only today thoroughly accustomed to this mode of communication but is actually rather comfortable with it. Within time, however, enthusiastic vice-chancellors saw electronic networks as providing a solution to at least two of their financial problems: the cost of buying printed materials for their university libraries, and of paying the salaries of university lecturers to stand in front of students and teach them. The number of students in higher educa-

tion in the UK has doubled in the 1990s. Teaching costs have
risen as a result of this rapidly growing student population and
senior managers of higher education institutions are constantly
looking for more cost-effective ways of controlling them.

The solution takes many forms but, essentially, material will
be stored within the university's electronic network and students
will proceed to the library where they can call up a book, a chapter,
or a paper on the computer screen and from there, read and
Learn. The most recent Government-funded enquiry into the future
of university libraries – the Follett Report – envisaged the library
as being the hub of the university in the future, not as a place to
go and read books and journals, but as a place to graze electronically through a plethora of material (under the guidance and
direction of the librarian), immediately available through a few
strikes on the keyboard. The problem and cost of buying multiple copies of books for the libraries would be solved, as indeed
would be the growing salary bills entailed in employing more
lecturers to teach an increasing student population.

This, of course, has been easier said than done because most
publishers balk at the idea of selling just one copy of a book to a
university which will then scan and store it and electronically
use it many times over. Neither are they very happy about being
asked to give permission for multiple photocopies of just one
chapter of a book which will end up in a specially compiled volume
of many such photocopied chapters, called in the UK course readers
or packs, and made available by the universities to their students
at a cheap price. Both the course pack and the electronically stored
book allow the user to 'pick and mix'. Control of copyright, therefore, has become a real issue over which both sides continue to
argue. One can safely predict, as publishers are essentially prag-
matists, that an agreement will eventually be reached over these
two major developments. However, both of them appear to signal
the end of a fundamental respect for the unity of the book.

SOME HISTORY

Looking back over the last twenty years of academic publishing,
perhaps what is happening today was inevitable. Anyone who
entered academic publishing in the 1970s will look back on that
era as a splendid one. The higher education sector was continually

expanding, and its budgets could support book buying on a scale that kept publishers in a healthy profit. This profit produced three main effects. The first was that being in relative good health, publishers did have the space to be creative and to take risks – to publish unusual but not necessarily profitable books which would add something quite distinctive to a subject area. Second, young editors were trained in an atmosphere in which learning to edit books was considered to be a long-drawn-out process, with knowledge and experience in depth being acquired over many years. Third, the profits allowed publishers to enter new subject areas, essentially developed in the universities and poly-technics which were founded in the 1960s and 70s. It was a genu-inely exciting time to be in academic publishing.

However, all good things often do come to an end and the end was signalled by a gradual decline in the book-buying budgets of the higher education institutions. The public purse could not support continual expansion, indeed it had to retrench. Publish-ers witnessed declining sales and were left with a financial prob-lem: how to maintain (indeed to grow) the turnover base at a time when sales for individual books were declining. The response was to publish more books. Crudely expressed, if one could publish more books – even with a decline in sales per title – one could end up with the same amount of turnover, or more; a situation, it seemed, infinitely preferable to the alternative, which was to reduce publishing programmes, turn away many hopeful authors and make staff redundant.

The situation was exacerbated in the 1980s by the growth of corporate publishing. There were literally dozens of imprints that were taken over, eventually to be merged within large corpora-tions. Not only was the individuality of those imprints lost, but their books, authors and titles were caught up in the financial imperatives of very large publishing conglomerates whose view on turnover and profit was, for academic publishing anyway, at best unrealistic and at worst, disastrous. Caught up in the drive to expand turnover and profit, editors found themselves required to commission books on a level which would have shocked editors whose careers in publishing had ended in the 1970s and early 80s. Whereas, formerly, an active and experienced editor would have been expected to commission 20–25 books a year, in recent years requirements of 40–50 books have been fairly common. One is leaving aside here editors who specialize in publishing academic monographs, where comparatively little creative work is required, and are expected to commission 70 titles or more a year.

This is a phenomenal workload for any editor, and what can one expect from any editor put in that situation? The owners and senior management of these publishing houses do expect miracles. They expect their editors to produce good quality books that will sell, to conceive new ideas for developing markets and developing formats, and their young and comparatively inexperienced editors to mature both as publishers and as financial managers of the destiny of their own lists at a pace which is possibly damaging. It is very difficult indeed for any young editor to acquire in-depth knowledge and experience of his or her profession and at the same time to juggle with the financial requirements of the organization, especially, it would seem, if the latter is more important than the former. So threats to respect for the book have come from within publishing, too, and it would be dishonest for any publisher to claim that it is all the fault of someone else!

Another significant factor is also making its presence felt. As a result of the new formula for the funding of higher education in the UK, universities can receive 'points' which will have a bearing on the total resources received from the government in any given year. There are many elements in this funding formula but an important one is the number of publications produced by the academic staff of an institution. For financial reasons, therefore, there is a growing pressure to publish coming from within the universities. Add to this the growing employment insecurity for academics, with tenure no longer an absolute given – bringing with it a pressing necessity to publish for careerist reasons – and publishers' lists begin to look like grossly overheated assembly lines rolling out more and more books intended to preserve the tenuous security of publishers and academia.

THE TRUTH ABOUT PUBLISHING

The truth is that it was ever thus. Publishers and authors have always been thoroughly opportunistic, pragmatically looking for chances to create extra sales. Even in expansionist and creative times, publishers' lists have carried so-so books, good-enough books, and, frankly, a number of bad books. There have always been exceptional editors persistently holding the line and who can be counted on to publish the books we admire. The number of authors capable of writing outstanding and influential books is quite small but it is their books we remember and, by extension, it is their work which we associate with the book, the vehicle which brought it to us. But to claim that all that is good has come to us via the book is a nonsense.

Publishing is, like any other organization, a victim of 'progress' – the scale becomes larger and the pace quickens. In that sense it reflects what is going on in the world around us and in a free market, we cannot stop it. As has been said many times before, the printed book succeeded not just because everyone agreed that this was a thoroughly clever invention but because it was a brilliant artefact which happened to suit the social and cultural conditions of a Europe emerging from the Middle Ages. Already inventions brought to us via technology have failed, or succeeded not quite in the overwhelming fashion that their developers claimed. Publishers have had their fingers burned with interactive media, money has been lost in the development of some CD-ROMs, and who now remembers microfiche, an invention of the early 1980s predicted to revolutionize our attitude to book buying? No one, including publishers, should fall for a variation of the Naturalistic Fallacy: because a product has been invented, people will want it.

People will want the products of digitization if they perceive them as superior in content and usage to what has gone before. There are books, even those containing reference material, which are still more efficient to use than their equivalent reformatted for computer technology. Turn to the back of a book which has a good index, then flick to the relevant pages and the reader can find what he or she needs rather more quickly than the process of entering a computer program and calling up entries under various field names. The sophistication and complexity of some software programs often leaves the users feeling overwhelmed with the 'riches' thrown at them. And there are times when the market simply does not want the riches assembled in some electronic products because it cannot perceive the advantage in possessing them – something which the producers clearly did not take into account, mistakenly believing that technology itself could drive market demand.

But there are many products, which were traditionally presented to us via the book, whose usefulness has been extended tremendously by their conversion into digitized form, and there are yet others who simply could not be encompassed by the book format. Other developments, for example, computerized library catalogues which enable the reader to enter a single word, such as 'existentialism', and call up onto the screen every book dealing with the subject, have been a boon to readers. Finally, whereas there are readers/users who feel most comfortable with a book in their hands, there are others – especially young people who have grown up with computers – who find sitting at a screen as normal as reading a book.

INFORMATION OR KNOWLEDGE?

The essential problem that lies behind the anxiety around the future of the book is that of confusing information with knowledge, and perhaps that very anxiety begs another, bigger question about the future of education. The future of education lies beyond the scope of this contribution, but for the moment, anyway, let us test the reality of the current status of the academic book at a time when many people would have us believe that its future will be short-lived. Setting aside what is on offer in the technological marketplace as vehicles for authors and publishers, this analysis will dwell on social, cultural and practical factors and how they determine what goes on and what might be, because culture changes far more slowly than technology does.

Without question, the prime objective of higher education is to instil knowledge and a sense of critical enquiry amongst students and those who teach them. Acquiring information may be a significant contribution to that process, but what one does with that information – how one interprets and analyses it – is still dependent on the skills that come from knowledge and understanding. For that, one needs the guidance of an expert – an author. The need for guidance from an expert to help interpret existing knowledge and understanding is even more pressing. The structure of the book and the conventions of prose writing are still the most convenient, flexible and comfortable way for the author to reflect on ideas and arguments, and for the reader to absorb those reflections. The book is as yet unbeatable as a vehicle for disseminating knowledge and for provoking considered thought. Digital technology would appear to be unbeatable as a storage archive but one should not confuse the two. Unfortunately, at the extreme edges of support for both these vehicles are those who insist on promoting the one at the expense of the other.

THE RISE, AND RISE, OF THE ACADEMIC AUTHOR

For academic publishers ruminating on the future for the book, there are dangers in overlooking the authors themselves. The academic author (almost inevitably a university or college lecturer) is most likely to be the prime consumer of academic books and through 'Recommended Reading' lists, the most influential promoter of academic books to the student market. With the growth of authorship amongst academics, these same authors have a vested interest in keeping the book going! It is not so much the prospect of fat royalty cheques that encourages them but the bearing that a well-reviewed and much-read book will have on their career paths, and their pride. It is not unknown these days in the UK for authors with a strong track-record in book authorship to be head-hunted for senior positions in our universities. For with them will come their points earned for each book published, and those points mean funding prizes. Negotiations take place over which books the academic will leave behind as points for the university he or she is leaving, and which books can be carried forward into their new posts. Book authorship is a very serious business indeed.

But there are other, less spoken about, factors. Authorial pride (not to say vanity) is as great amongst academic authors as any other writers. The sheer spitefulness of academic reviewing in the UK is witness to the extent that academics really do care (even in a seemingly negative way) about what is written about in books. Scratch the surface of a piqued author or a reviewer (also, inevitably, an author), and one is as likely to find hurt pride as outrage at someone else's claim to superior scholarship.

Add to this prestige. Although the market in authors has grown, prestige has not diminished, evidenced by the second most frequent question asked by an author of a publisher after question number one: 'When is publication date?' That question is, 'Can I have a launch party?' Launch parties in academic publishing used to be comparatively rare, and usually it was the publisher who thought one might be appropriate. Today, when publishers compare notes, they are often found complaining to each other that all authors these days seem to think that a launch party would be both appropriate and desirable. This is not the moment to discuss the merits of these parties, but certainly, something is going on and the highly symbolic nature of a launch party suggests that both status and prestige play an important part in all this.

Academic authorship has grown tremendously in the last ten years in the UK. There is scarcely a half-decent academic around who by now has not written a book. One could argue that the average author, stuck in the endless sausage machine of the growing output of publishers, at worst craves the launch party as a desperate means of conveying that he or she has done something special, or at best, genuinely feels that the new book should be celebrated, and these days, feels less frightened of publishers to ask for one. Whatever the reasons, there are a lot of academic authors out there, and more on their way (I know of no publisher who is experiencing a decline in submissions) and they have many reasons for wishing to see the book prosper.

THE FUTURE

What publishers will choose to do with these submissions is another matter, of course. Publishers, following current and anticipating future trends in the core of their marketplace, can drive authors out and can also drive authors into types of publication that they may not have considered before. There are authors now writing textbooks in their subjects which they would not have considered, nor indeed would have approved of, in the past. British higher education, until comparatively recently, was not at all textbook oriented. Students were encouraged to read as widely as possible, usually supplementary texts (discursive by nature) and journal articles (offering the most current research). However, both publishers and lecturers alike are more than aware that today's financially pressed student is not able to purchase anything more than the bare minimum of books and the textbook holds attractions for them. Even if 'blue riband' academics demur at the thought of writing textbooks, there are plenty of other authors ready to do so and, frankly, it is often the middle-of-the-road, 'hands on' academic who is perceived by the publisher to be the ideal author for this kind of publication.

Meanwhile, in every academic publishing house in the land, the cry has gone out to editors to give those only-adequately-performing supplementary texts short shrift and to concentrate on textbooks because this is where sure sales lie. Textbook publishing, of course, is highly competitive and many publishers will lose only in the tooth-and-nail fight to get their books posted on students' reading lists as compulsory or recommended reading. And if publishers are not pushing for textbooks, they are pushing for collections: edited volumes of many contributions, which can be put together very quickly and, in the spread of authorship, can act as a quasi-textbook and possess the beauty of being assembled and brought to the marketplace far quicker than a single or joint-authored book. Ten years ago, most reputable publishers were quite snooty about these edited collections but, as ever, publishers have jettisoned their prejudices and followed their pragmatic instincts.

What will happen to all these supplementary texts, traditionally the means through which the academic authors bring their scholarship to the market? It is inconceivable to think that the major academic publishing houses will jettison them in a wholesale fashion in order to concentrate entirely on publishing textbooks. Textbooks, after all, are for students. University lecturers have to read altogether less simplified and more original material in order to maintain their own standards of scholarship in their chosen subject area. No university lecturer can expect to meet the requirements of career and academic advancement, or to attain the much-needed status of author, through reading textbooks. There is an ongoing need for these books which publishers must satisfy. Even if the major houses do cut down on the number of supplementary texts they publish, and increasingly concentrate on textbooks, commercial and business sense suggest that whereas successful textbook publishing does offer the promise of tremendous financial rewards, this kind of publishing is inherently risky because it is so competitive. These houses could be punished commercially, and very easily, if they put all their eggs in one basket. It will make sense, therefore, even for the big houses to keep a presence in supplementary text publishing. It is more stable and it benefits from the interlocking relationship between the market of academic authorship and publishers which was described earlier.

There is another factor in favour of the supplementary text.

These books have a potential international readership. Textbooks do not travel well, structured as they are to meet the needs of the domestic student market. In any subject area, the further one travels along the continuum of knowledge and research, the sooner one finds oneself in an international constituency of scholarship anxious to acquaint itself with the latest developments in theory and research from all around the world. Scholarly journals are not just the source for finding out about these developments; so are supplementary texts and all publishers these days rely on international sales to keep themselves in good financial health.

Finally, one must remember that publishing houses change and evolve. Whenever large publishing houses, which dominate the scene, change their character and withdraw from certain areas which they once regarded as their bread and butter, their place in those areas is often taken by smaller (sometimes new) houses who seize the opportunities that come when space is made available for them. The small house is not tied to the kind of overheads which the large houses have to carry and can often drive them into 'safe' publishing. This is true not just of academic publishing but also of general publishing. In the UK it has often been remarked in recent years that some of the most interesting and vigorous publishing to be found has emerged from relatively small houses whose financial imperatives are more flexible and whose owners and managers perceive that the only way forward for them is to remain individualistic.

It would be thoroughly unfair, and indeed misleading, to suggest that smaller houses will be the torchbearers for the traditional book – there are still prestigious and pathbreaking books being published by the very large houses, and many editors in them hellbent on keeping it that way – but taking the activities of both these players on the academic publishing scene together, it is stretching the imagination and the credulity of both readers and writers to suggest that the book truly is under threat.

REAL THREATS

The worst threats are often the ones we do not see coming until they are upon us. Futurology is always a risky business, combining as it does the temptation to exaggerate current developments with a 'vision' that seems scarcely credible, and often hellish, to

the ordinary person. One sometimes wonders if the real function of gurus who predict that in ten years time the book will be
dead, that we shall somehow be intravenously wired up to digital technology and that our only sense of meaning will be through
visual spatiality, is to irritate us and impel us to fight to keep
the things that we value as they are.

What we can keep will be a matter of social and cultural forces
and of politics. At the same time as this book is being written,
there are in the UK no real signs that readership is on the de-
crease. Bookshops are very busy and lively places. Reading groups
are on the increase. The country is poised for a huge campaign
to promote literacy. This campaign has come about from the combined concerns of the educational, business and governmental
communities and it is regarded as equally as important as teaching children and adults to be conversant and effective with the
new technologies. That in itself is quite interesting. It signals not
just that it is imperative that people are able to do basic reading
and writing but that both are the key to enhancing many aspects of one's life. Perhaps that is what we should be concen-
trating on – reading and writing as a critical means for everyone
– instead of a hopeless battle over the relative merits of the book
versus digital technology. There is a place for both as long as we
can remember what each is best at doing for us. Even e-mail has
revived a letter writing of sorts!

There is, however, a threat to books and authorship which comes
from half-veiled, and sometimes fully blown, attacks on copyright. As was mentioned earlier, UK universities want to scan,
store, download, and sometimes reproduce in modified form,
published material. To write something, and therefore to own
and to control what one has written, is a very important matter
to anyone who has laboured not just over words but over, perhaps, half-a-lifetime's accumulation of knowledge and experience,
to produce something which may bring some financial reward
but, more importantly, brings the unique voice of the author's
scholarship and ideas to the reader. Ironically, it is from within
the home of scholarship that the greatest threat to the authority
of copyright, and therefore authorship, has come.

The response of the universities seems rational put in terms of
resourcing difficulties, and perhaps part of the anger sometimes
directed at publishers is because they believe that publishing is
taking a high-handed position, refusing to understand their

financial problems and help ease the situation by being less
transigent about a freer use of copyright material. The arguments,
however, are not simply about money (that is the fees that might
be charged for scanning, storing and downloading books); they
are also fundamentally about preserving the status and unity of
the book, and of authorship. Publishers still do not see themselves as being in the business of creating a body of words, which
for the moment we can call a book, which on release is then
available at a price for a third party to cannibalize and redistrib-
ute as they see fit. And one doubts very much if that is what
authors want either. There is an inherent nonsense in the notion
of writing a whole book just to see parts of it appear in edited
'highlights'. There is a decided difference between this kind of
exercise in deconstruction and compilation and the edited collection where contributors are asked to write a chapter on one
particular issue, as part of a whole (such as this book), or where
a series of journal articles are put together, again to create a whole.
In the latter two cases, the contributions are discrete entities: they
can stand on their own and the author has written them with
precisely that intention.

IN CONCLUSION

Books and authorship are wholly linked and the health of both
are dependent on each other. It seems such an obvious thing to
say, and yet it does need to be restated at a time when the possibilities exist for the fruits of authorship to be absorbed and dis-
tributed in ways that the author never intended. There is a huge
amount of work in print ready, if publishers were to give permission, to be scanned and reassembled for teaching use, but if
new books are to be written, guarantees must exist which preserve the copyright on the material and safeguard for the author
his or her ability to control what happens to it. If the risks of
authorship seem too high, then what price the book?

No doubt the heady rush to try to make full use of the potential of digital technology, which crashed head on with publishers
anxious to protect not just their publications but also their authors,
will subside into an atmosphere better informed by realism. Publishers, already, are talking about digital technology being not a
threat but an opportunity and some licences are already in place

which will allow users to scan and download material. Similarly, universities must come to terms with the protection of authors (usually their own employees) and their work. Eventually, another kind of partnership will be worked out between consumer and producer if the product, for which there is demand, is to survive. There is no real hard evidence that universities wish to sideline the role of publishers, sifting and sorting new material and deciding what should be made available, and then taking on what is often the more onerous task of distributing it. And if they did, they would probably end up behaving just like publishers!

In the meantime, perhaps implicit in this ongoing debate is a recognition that there is something worth fighting over – the fruits of authorship. Whatever happens next, the supreme vehicle for authorship – the book – would appear to be alive and in relatively good shape. As was ever the case in academic publishing, we may disapprove sometimes of what is brought to the marketplace and disagree whether it represents real scholarship; we may also have great misgiving about the internal financial pressures of publishing houses which has changed the nature of editorial work; and we may feel some dismay at the increasingly polarization between large houses and their drive towards textbooks and smaller houses busily trying to remain individualistic but yet lacking the sheer muscle power of their big competitors to dominate the market. But as much as there is an evolution taking place, there is undoubtedly still vigour there, as evidenced by the contents of publishers' catalogues. The academic book will remain alive and well provided authors are protected by copyright and until the book's supreme efficacy in transmitting knowledge and understanding is superseded by something else.

19

The End of the Book?
Some Perspectives on
Media Change

ELIZABETH L. EISENSTEIN

'Closing the Book on Books' – so ran a headline in the *Washington Post* in December 1995 over a review (by Jonathan Yardley) of Sven Birkerts' *The Gutenberg Elegies*. Author and reviewer agree that similar dirges have become increasingly frequent. Birkerts cites Alvin Kernan's *Death of Literature* as a case in point. Kernan, in turn, mentions many other relevant titles. In the 1960s, electronic mass media, radio, film, and television were singled out as being chiefly responsible for the book's demise. At present we are more likely to hear about personal computers, data banks, and cyberspace. But however varied the diagnosis, the gloomy prognosis remains much the same.

'The demanding world of reading is being shoved aside in favor of the easy one of audio and video,' writes Yardley. Birkerts' formulation is more grandiose and sweeping:

As Marshall McLuhan originally theorized (and as Kernan has reaffirmed) we are in the midst of an epoch-making transition; ... the societal shift from print-based to electronic communications is as consequential for culture as was the shift instigated by Gutenberg's invention of movable type. ... If this fact has not yet struck home ... it is, in part, because the news of the change is still being delivered slowly, piecemeal, by way of the entrenched agencies of print. This circuit-driven renovation is happening in every sector on every level and the momentum will not slacken until the electronic web has woven itself into every potentially profitable crevice. Ten, fifteen years from now the world will be nothing like what we remember, nothing much like what we experience now. . . . Our relationship to the space-time axis will be very different from what we have lived with for millennia.

It should be noted that we have not lived with the printed book 'for millennia' or even for one millennium. During the centuries that ensued after Gutenberg's invention, moreover, our experience of 'space-time' has scarcely remained unchanged. Indeed the feeling of being 'in the midst of an epoch-making transition' serves to link our generation with several that have gone before. In 1836, Alfred de Musset described how his generation experienced the aftermath of the French Revolution and the Napoleonic wars: 'behind them, a past forever destroyed; before them, the first gleams of the future and between these two worlds . . . a troubled sea filled with wreckage . . . in a word: the present.' Later on, Henry Adams wrote about being abruptly severed from the experience of his ancestors by the Boston and Albany Railroad, the first Cunard steamer, and the stringing of telegraph wires. In the early twentieth century, Samuel Eliot Morison said the same thing about the internal combustion engine, nuclear fission, and Dr. Freud.

Is the idea that a new age has dawned with the advent of new media also embedded in our past? To place current attitudes in some sort of historical perspective, it may be helpful to consider reactions to previous changes affecting media. I have recently been surveying such reactions, beginning with early comments on the advent of movable type. For the sake of brevity, this essay will set aside the first centuries of printing and will consider only the later interval that saw steam-powered iron machinery replace the wooden handpress.

The industrialization of papermaking and the use of iron cylinder presses harnessed to steam (first used by the *London Times* in 1814) provoked much comment. For the most part, however, the new machinery led to the use of new metaphors rather than to any major alteration of previous themes. Although printing was more likely to be described as a 'mighty engine of progress' than as a 'divine art' in the nineteenth century, it was still regarded by both its friends and enemies in much the same way as it had been during previous centuries. To be sure, attitudes were sharply polarized, but this was less because of the industrialization of papermaking and printing than because of the political upheavals associated with the Atlantic revolutions.

In his reassertion of the principles of the Declaration of the Rights of Man of 1789, Tom Paine attacked Edmund Burke for 'laboring in vain to stop the progress of knowledge.' 'It has never yet been discovered how to make a man unknow his knowledge or unthink his thoughts.' 'Ignorance is of a peculiar nature; once dispelled it is impossible to reestablish it.' Paine's views were shared by his friends among the French revolutionaries, such as Condorcet, who placed Gutenberg's invention at the beginning of a new world historical age. Printing, the revolutionaries agreed, had set in motion an irreversible process that was destined to end a royal monopoly of power as well as a priestly monopoly of learning. This position was adopted by most of the early nineteenth-century opponents of Metternich and the Bourbon Restoration. Societies for press freedom were formed; all of the written constitutions that were proposed by Liberal parties throughout the Continent during the nineteenth century reasserted the freedom of the press clause in the 1789 Declaration of the Rights of Man. The cause of a free press became a liberal shibboleth (and remains one even now).

At the opposite pole were the conservatives and reactionaries who supported the so-called party of order. They regarded the Enlightenment as a prelude to the Terror and held printing responsible for the spread of poisonous Jacobinical and atheistical doctrines. The Catholic Church, which had viewed printing with suspicion ever since Luther's day, took the lead in opposing doctrines favoring freedom of opinion and of the press. In 1791 when the Pope denounced the Civil Constitution of the Clergy he singled out the freedom of the press clause in the Declaration of the Rights of Man and the Citizen for special condemnation. Since God had limited man's liberty by forbidding him to commit evil, the papal argument went, liberty of thought was wrongly described as an imprescriptible right. This position was emphatically reiterated later in the century by Pius IX in his Syllabus of Errors of 1864, which pronounced anathema against every doctrine that was cherished by nineteenth-century liberals.

Long before the 1860s, however, the Catholic royalist reaction had received a decisive setback in France. The high-water mark was reached in 1830 when Charles X (the last Bourbon king) issued the repressive Four Ordinances, one of which was aimed at closing down the newspaper and periodical press. These measures set off the July Revolution, which saw printers and journalists playing prominent roles and which resulted in the accession of Louis Philippe, the Orleanist king.

As a constitutional monarch, Louis Philippe tried, unsuccessfully, to find a middle path between Right and Left. In 1792, he fought on the side of the revolutionaries at Valmy and Jemappes. His anti-clerical views linked him with the Voltaireans. He also agreed with the views of Condorcet on printing and its effects. Writing in the 1800s while traveling in America, the future Citizen King described the advent of printing as the most decisive of all historical events. It had undermined feudalism and advanced equality, he wrote, adding that 'the European governments are operating under a delusion if they think that they can hold back the irreversible changes printing is bringing in its wake.'

Once he was made king, however, Louis Philippe endured the attacks of republicans and ultra royalists alike for only a few years before he felt obliged to reinstitute press controls. But Orleanist press laws proved difficult to enforce. As had been the case in Georgian England in the days of John Wilkes, trials by jury often resulted in the vindication of the accused and invariably led to publicity unfavorable to the beleaguered government. When the Orleanists were overthrown in 1848, the staffs of two journals took over the provisional government of France, and freedom of the press was once again proclaimed – only to give way to new press controls under Napoleon III.

Not until the collapse of the Second Empire and the installation of the Third Republic in the 1870s did the struggle over press laws end in favor of the anti-clerical Liberals. In the 1870s, Liberal parties elsewhere on the Continent were victorious. The last decades of the nineteenth century saw the movement for a free press finally prevail. This was a mixed blessing in the somewhat jaundiced view of Carlton J. H. Hayes, the professor of history at Columbia who was a Catholic convert and who became U.S. ambassador to Franco's Spain. In *A Generation of Materialism, 1871–1900*, Hayes described how a free press, mass literacy, and popular journalism went together with bellicose nationalism, imperialist adventures, and ever more destructive wars. (It should be noted, however, that the cause of peace has scarcely advanced when press controls have been reinstituted by totalitarian regimes.)

On the Continent, Enlightenment doctrines that favored printing as an instrument of progress were associated with the struggle against clerical influence. Across the Channel, contestation took a somewhat different form. There the revolutionary aftermath had seen a Tory government impose new heavy duties on paper and periodicals. Enlightenment themes were revitalized, and the praise of printing took on new life as philosophical radicals, liberal reformers, book publishers, and newspaper editors combined to campaign against the Tory taxes.

The stark contrast between ignorance and knowledge that had been drawn by Tom Paine was repeatedly evoked in the campaign. Taxes on printed materials were described as 'taxes on knowledge,' and a Society for the Promotion of Useful Knowledge was formed. Working-class leaders and middle-class reformers together insisted that free access to the printed word was indispensable to the welfare of the nation. Benthamites and Malthusians were especially zealous on this point. They believed that ignorance was chiefly responsible for the misery of the laboring poor and that education was the best remedy for the nation's ills. Once they had been taught about the principles of population, workers would understand the need for family planning and exhibit more self-control. Even alcoholism could be eliminated, it was argued, when the public's thirst for news could be required without workingmen having to go to taverns to look at newspapers.

By 1836 the heavy duties had been reduced, a legal penny press came into existence, and middle-class members of the Useful Knowledge society were satisfied. But working-class spokesmen found that their illegal untaxed operations suffered from competition with the new legal penny press. It made the rich man's paper cheaper but the poor man's paper dearer, according to complaints. Leaders of the Chartist movement continued to campaign for a completely unstamped press. In doing so, the Chartists perpetuated Enlightenment slogans. Henry Hetherington, editor of the *Poor Man's Guardian*, for example, defiantly substituted for the official red stamp a black one, which bore the emblem of a handpress and was inscribed with the epigraph KNOWLEDGE IS POWER.

This use of Francis Bacon's seventeenth-century phrase shows how attitudes that had been shaped in the age of the handpress tended to be perpetuated in the age of new machinery. In *Sartor Resartus*, Thomas Carlyle, in his inimitable style, reasserted the views of Condorcet. He who first shortened the labors of copyists by the device of movable type, wrote Carlyle, was disbanding hired armies, cashiering most kings, and creating a whole new democratic world. In 1843, Charles Dickens described printing as the only product of civilization that was necessary to the existence of free men. The press, he said, was the fountain of knowledge, the bulwark of freedom, the founder and preserver of free states.

Carlyle opposed the extension of democracy, and Dickens expressed bitter thoughts about feeding a relentless machine. When sounding alarms about the effects of increased output, nineteenth-century commentators were still playing variations on long-familiar themes. Concern about the sheer proliferation of printed matter and about markets clogged with useless materials had been expressed in previous centuries. In the seventeenth century, Sir Thomas Browne complained that too many books were being produced simply 'to benefit the trade and mystery of typographers.' In the next century, Alexander Pope presented his apocalyptic vision of the flood of printer's ink that was spreading darkness across the land.

Nevertheless, statistics were on the side of those who felt victimized by an unprecedented onslaught of trash after industrialization. 'The tawdry novels, hideous and ignoble, which flare in the bookshelves of our railway stations' offended Matthew Arnold's sensibilities (much as the contents of airport bookshelves offend us right now). The late Victorian age, according to G. M. Young, saw a public, which had once been alert and responsible, sink toward an 'easily excited, easily satisfied state of barbarism and childhood' – a sorry state that was fostered by an irresponsible press.

The notion that the press might contribute to barbarism, outbreaks of war fever, and childlike ignorance presented a sharp contrast to the expectations of members of the Useful Knowledge society. For the most part, nineteenth-century liberals continued to pin their hopes on improvements in printing processes and on the continued expansion of a reading public. John Stuart Mill worried about the effect of a mass market on traditional values, about the spread of conformity, the abuses of literacy, and the estrangement of the intellectual. Yet he also welcomed all 'the modern facilities of communication' and never doubted the value of institutions that guaranteed freedom of the press.

Some nineteenth-century observers regarded the proliferation of printed materials as a mixed blessing. Others viewed it with less ambivalence as an unmitigated curse. Opponents of the Enlightenment and the French Revolution looked with special favor on those very distant golden ages that were untroubled by the output of printers. Conservatives and reactionaries expressed a new appreciation of preliterate folkways, unwritten laws, oral myths, and legends. Catholic royalists valued medieval cathedrals, manuscript illumination, and monkish scribes. Indeed, many of the cultural artefacts that were celebrated during the Gothic revival had been uncontaminated by print.

In his *Reflections on the Revolution in France*, Edmund Burke had complained that the age of chivalry was dead: 'The age of chivalry is gone. That of sophisters, economists and calculators has succeeded and the glory of Europe is extinguished forever.' Soon thereafter the age of chivalry received a literary resurrection in the novels of Sir Walter Scott. Among Scott's many Continental admirers, the young Victor Hugo deserves special mention for his celebrated discussion of printing and its effects. An entire chapter is devoted to the topic in Hugo's *Notre Dame de Paris*. The Gothic cathedral with its magnificent stained glass and stone sculpture is set in that novel against the printed dictionary, and the reader is invited to lament the triumph of pedantry over poetry.

What the utilitarians viewed as useful knowledge was scornfully dismissed as shallow and one-dimensional by a new generation of romantics who were steeped in German philosophy and valued the imaginative visionary above the precise engineer. Dry-as-dust pedants or petty bookkeepers might pride themselves on their mastery of facts and figures; deeper truths were available to those who tapped the wellsprings of folk wisdom. But not even folk wisdom could escape the intrusion of market values; cheap editions of twice-told tales that had once circulated in the form of ballads were being recycled and rewritten for mass consumption, ultimately degenerating into kitsch. Once the aristocratic patron had been displaced, a cash nexus contaminated all aesthetic endeavors, or so it was held.

At the same time, the flourishing state of print culture in the nineteenth century enabled the author to achieve unprecedented popularity as a new culture hero. One thinks of the people waiting on the dock to learn about the fate of Little Nell or the worshipful crowds walking behind Victor Hugo's hearse. (Do recent verdicts on the 'death of the author' merely imply that no author's funeral will ever again be so well attended?) Carlyle's 'hero as a man of letters' with his 'copy rights and copy wrongs' was a by-product of those very same impersonal market forces that most authors claimed to despise. The fortunes of the serialized fiction writer, for example, hinged on the new technology employed by newspaper publishers. But nineteenth-century literati continued to wax nostalgic for bardic poets, scribal arts, and noble patrons. Even while feeding the voracious machine, they denounced it with all the fury of the Luddite.

Perhaps the most damning description of print culture in an industrial age was offered by Balzac's *Les Illusions Perdues*. The novel begins with a view of the world turned upside down by the French Revolution. First a nobleman and then a priest are forced to toil for an illiterate peasant turned provincial printer. The latter makes a fortune during the Terror by employing his former masters as hired hands. The old villain is too much of a skinflint to equip his presses properly. He accumulates money by hoarding and by starving the members of his household. (The portrait is not dissimilar from that drawn by Erasmus of Aldus Manutius's miserly father-in-law, the publisher Andrea Torresani of Asola.) The scene then moves to the great city of Paris, which is depicted as a kind of hell with market forces viewed in a lurid light. The miserly artisan with his wooden handpress has been left behind in the provinces. In Paris, the iron laws of capitalism have taken hold. Publishers investing in meretricious bestsellers protect their investments by bribery and blackmail. They arrange for corrupt critics to praise worthless books and to denounce or ignore praiseworthy ones. They force poor authors to choose between slavery to the system or starving on their own.

Balzac's portrayal of conniving publishers and desperate Grub Street authors is too often taken at face value as a realistic rendering of the literary marketplace in nineteenth-century Paris. Some allowance needs to be made for the author's personal experience as a failed printer and publisher and also for the partisan politics of the day. Balzac was a lifelong admirer of Sir Walter Scott. One of his first successful novels, *Les Chouans*, glorified a counter-revolutionary uprising.

The long history of friction between authors and publishers also needs to be taken into account. From the days of Erasmus down to the present, there is scarcely any writer who has not at one time or another expressed detestation of the cold-blooded, calculating, profit-seeking publisher who wrings the last penny from starving writers while hastily marketing inferior goods. It is interesting to note that there are references in *Illusions Perdues* to a distant golden age of handpress printing when Aldus Manutius, the Estiennes, and the Elseviers plied their trade. Here as elsewhere the nineteenth-century romantic imagination tended to set the best of the past against the worst of the present – to exaggerate the role of the aristocratic patron and to play down the market forces that affected literature before industrialization.

Horror stories about the greed and knavery of early printers and publishers are not difficult to find. Along with Aldus's miserly father-in-law, another celebrated early printer, the pioneering atlas publisher, W. J. Blaeu (who was associated with the dawn of the so-called golden age of Dutch publishing) provoked a contemporary to complain: 'He sets more store by his own good than by the general good, is more concerned for gold than for honor, and thinks of nothing but profit.' The Elseviers, perhaps the last to represent the Dutch golden age, were frequently accused of harsh dealings – in one instance, of letting a widow and orphan starve. The Dutch were especially likely targets for such accusations. They had been caricatured during the Anglo-Dutch wars as dull accountants and avaricious merchants. The caricature was reinforced by eighteenth-century French literati who resented having to deal with extraterritorial publishers. The mythical Amsterdam publisher who did not know how to read but made millions from Frenchmen who knew how to write was immortalized by Voltaire.

In the days of Voltaire, artisans were still manning wooden presses and papermaking had not yet been mechanized. Yet literati were still convinced that they were witnessing the onset of an iron age of commercialism. It is noteworthy that the historian Robert Darnton finds that Balzac's portrayal fits eighteenth-century publishing, although the conniving publishers and desperate hacks in Darnton's studies belong to the pre-revolutionary and pre-industrial age. There is little to differentiate Darnton's description of the cut-throat business of publishing from Balzac's, except that Darnton's publishers work outside French borders and Balzac's are more concerned with receiving favorable notice in the Parisian daily press.

Mention of the daily press brings up one development that deserves special treatment. Up to this point, I have followed one of Carlyle's essays and dealt with a 'huge froth ocean of printed speech loosely called literature' without distinguishing between books and newspapers. Such distinctions seem relatively unimportant when considering such matters as cognitive progress, popularization, and censorship. To be sure, publishers were less likely to be prosecuted for costly volumes aimed at elites than for cheap papers that presumably stirred up the rabble. Yet efforts to control all printed output characterized authoritarian regimes in the past and still mark totalitarian regimes in the present century. Nineteenth-century liberals objected to the Index of Prohibited Books as well as to censorship of periodicals and newspapers. (A difficult book, not a readable pamphlet, has led to the death sentence imposed upon Salman Rushdie.) Furthermore, distinctions between books and periodicals were themselves often blurred by the publishing of books in installments and their serialization in newspapers.

Nevertheless, even a sketchy account must make room for the special niche occupied by journalism. Robert Owen described the newspaper as 'the most powerful engine for good or evil that has been brought into action by human creation.' John Stuart Mill, reflecting on the 'tyranny' exerted by public opinion, observed that the masses were no longer taking their opinions from dignitaries in Church or State. Nor were they being guided by books. 'Their thinking is done for them by men, much like themselves, through the newspapers.' Indeed, the end of the book was first proclaimed, not by recent commentators on electronic media, but by nineteenth-century critics of the newspaper press. In *The Decline of the West*, Oswald Spengler associated the invention of printing with the birth of Faustian Man. But he also asserted that, just as the age of the sermon had given way to the age of the book, so too the age of the book had in turn been superseded by the age of the newspaper. As we shall see, he was echoing previous observations made by Carlyle and Louis Blanc.

The increased significance assigned to the newspaper press owed much to improvements in papermaking and print technology as well as to the French Revolution, especially to the explosion of Parisian print journalism in 1789. But views of print journalism had also been shaped by developments that predate 1789 – going back at least to sixteenth-century Venice where Aretino, the so-called father of journalism, had pioneered in exploiting printed publicity for the purposes of blackmail. Satires on journalism were familiar to London playgoers in Ben Jonson's time. In the aftermath of the English Civil War, an official serving Charles II complained: 'The press makes the multitude too familiar with the actions and counsels of their superiors. . . . It gives them not only an itch but a kind of right and license to be meddling with the government.'

Two separate accounts – one written by a Frenchman, the other by a German – appeared in the early 1700s, proclaiming that the century of the journal had dawned. During the course of the eighteenth century, the trade of the journalist was often discussed, rarely in favorable terms. (At that time, the term *journalist* was subject to confusion since it designated the respectable editors of learned journals as well as the disreputable scandalmongers who traded in gossip and blackmail.) The philosophes were generally contemptuous. According to Diderot, journals were designed for readers too lazy to read books; journalism was 'a sad and servile trade.'

Among the radical political activists who admired John Wilkes, Sam Adams, and Tom Paine, however, the journalists were seen to pursue a higher calling as 'tribunes of the people.' For those who opposed George III, the newspaper press was 'the Tyrant's foe and the people's friend.' It was assigned the same sort of power over the public mind that television newscasts are assigned today. It was the ideal instrument for raising the consciousness of 'the nation outdoors.' Jacques Pierre Brissot asserted that 'without newspapers and gazettes, the American Revolution would never have occurred.' During the French Revolution, journalism served Brissot (and Mirabeau, Marat, Desmoulins, and many others) as a 'prelude to power.' In 1848, the same theme was replayed when the staffs of two journals took over the provisional government of France.

In the aftermath of the Atlantic revolutions, observers began to consider the possibility that the newspaper press constituted a new organ of the body politic. Probably the most influential phrasemaker in this regard was Thomas Carlyle, who wrote that journalists 'are now our true kings and clergy' and that 'the true Church of England lies in the editors of our newspapers.' Carlyle's most resonant passages on journalism occur in his *History of the French Revolution*, where he described the explosion of newsprint in the streets of Paris in 1789 in a section that began: 'Great is journalism; every able editor is now a ruler of the world.'

Carlyle's phrases were picked up and translated into French by Louis Blanc for use in his history of the French Revolution.

Writing after his own career as a journalist-turned-deputy had come to an end, Blanc produced a much-cited chapter on the emergence of journalism as a new power in human affairs. Books were suited to quieter times, he wrote, paraphrasing Carlyle, but we are now in an era when today devours yesterday and must be devoured by tomorrow. And then comes the celebrated formula: The age of books is closed; the age of the journal is at hand.

It was Carlyle, again, who attributed to Edmund Burke the idea that newspaper reporters belonged to a new Fourth Estate: 'Burke said that there were Three Estates in Parliament; but, in the Reporters' Gallery yonder, there sat a *fourth Estate* more import-ant far than they all. It is not a figure of speech, or a witty saying; it is a literal fact – very momentous to us in these times. . . . Whoever can speak, speaking now to the whole nation, becomes a power, a branch of government, with inalienable weight in law making, in all acts of authority.'

It is not certain whether Burke ever did point to the reporters' gallery and coin the phrase. But it certainly did catch on by the 1820s. It was repeatedly employed by liberal politicians such as Macaulay and Brougham and has remained current in Anglo-American parlance ever since those days. An American variation on the theme was supplied in the 1950s by the title of Douglass Cater's book *The Fourth Branch of Government*. Cater prefaced his work with an epigraph from James Reston: 'The nineteenth cen-tury was the era of the novelist. The twentieth century is the era of the journalist.' One wonders why observers in the Western world feel called on to make such pronouncements. From the days of Daniel Defoe to those of Norman Mailer, novelist and journalist have coexisted; not infrequently the same person has assumed both roles.

By the mid-nineteenth century, in any event, the journalist was already assuming a self-congratulatory posture. The idea of a Fourth Estate had been taken over by the leader writers for the *London Times*: 'Daily appealing to the enlightened force of public opinion; anticipating when possible the march of events, stand-ing upon the breach between past and future, extending its sur-vey to the horizon of the world, journalism was now truly an estate of the realm more powerful than any other estate' – so ran a *London Times* editorial of 1852. Some writers accepted this appraisal at face value; others made it a target for savage satire. In *Pendennis*, Thackeray described the awe inspired by passing a

London newspaper office at night with its lights ablaze: 'Look at that! There she is, the great engine who never sleeps. She has ambassadors in every quarter of the world; her couriers upon every road.'

Trollope managed to deflate the overblown pretensions of journalists in pages of mock epic prose: 'From Mount Olympus issued fourth 50,000 nightly edicts for the governance of the subject nation. Issued forth the only infallible bulls for the guidance of British souls and bodies. Self-nominated self-consecrated as pontiff, never wrong ever vigilant and all knowing, from the palaces of St Petersburg to the cabins of Connaught; nothing escapes him.' Readers (or viewers) of Trollope's *The Warden* will be familiar with inhumane and amoral behavior attributed to the reporter for the *London Times* (or the *Jupiter*, as Trollope called it). The power attributed to the newspaper by the novelist was entirely irresponsible. It was accountable to no one, except perhaps to the advertisers who hinged rates to circulation figures.

The emergence of an independent newspaper press, which provoked so much comment in the nineteenth century, was linked to the replacement of government subsidies by commercial advertising – a phenomenon well advanced in England before it caught on across the Channel and one that Tory ministers regarded with dismay. According to D.C. Somervell: 'In 1795 the publisher of the *Times* agreed to support the government for a pension of 600 pounds. His successor in 1815 would have laughed at such a proposal.' Somervell also takes note of Lord Liverpool's complaint to Castlereagh that no paper any longer accepted money from the government. When their support was most necessary, they could not be bribed. Instead of begging favors from the government, they had become sycophants of the public. Later, of course, radicals and socialists would argue that reliance on advertisers, far from guaranteeing the independence of the press, made it all the more dependent on the special interests of big business. To a twentieth-century Laborite, journals such as the *London Times* were sycophants not of the public but of corporate wealth.

The intrusion of commercial interests into literature, long bemoaned by literati, was especially galling to nineteenth-century fiction writers, who depended on newspaper publicity and found themselves competing for space, not only with headline-grabbing politicians, but also with vulgar commodities. In his preface to

Mademoiselle de Maupin (1835), Theophile Gautier expressed savage indignation at the idea of having his work advertised along with elastic belts, crinoline collars, patent nipple nursing bottles, and recipes for toothaches. He complained that the public's appetite for scandal was being so whetted by reports of sensational trials that 'the reader refuses to be caught save by a book baited with a small corpse in the first stages of putrefaction. Men are not as unlike fishes as some people seem to think.' Although many writers expressed disgust at the vulgar sensationalism of others, few could afford to abandon the hope of creating a sensation themselves.

Novelists were not alone in expressing concern about the effects of sensational journalism. Much as early printers had denounced one another for sharp dealing, so too did newspapers hurl accusations at one another: 'squirt of filthy water,' 'sloppail of corruption,' and other such epithets scarcely dignified the trade. Moralists persisted, as they had for centuries, deploring the public preference for the salacious over the edifying tale. And as is the case even now, doctors became alarmed over the deterioration of the nation's mental health. A physician named Isaac Ray published a book entitled *Mental Hygiene* in 1863, in which he asserted that 'no single incident of civilization has contributed so much to maintain the mental activity of modern times as the art of printing; and at no period since its invention have its benefits and its evils been more widely diffused.' Ray went on to express concern about the effects of this diffusion and noted, among other worries, the adverse effects of crime reporting on the national psyche: 'The details of a disgusting criminal trial, exposing the darkest aspects of our nature, find an audience that no court-room less than a hemisphere could hold.'

On such issues, nineteenth-century opinions and present-day attitudes do not seem far apart. Although different mass media are being targeted, the complaints are much the same: the ubiquity of sex and violence; intrusive commercials; sycophancy to mass taste; quasi-hypnotic power over human minds. The book is no longer seen to be succumbing to the newspaper (although it is still believed to be outmoded). It is now the newspaper's turn to succumb to television. Print journalism is already beginning to be viewed with the sort of nostalgia previously reserved for the early days of the wooden handpress – as the best of the past continues to be set against the worst of the present.

I've devoted considerable space to the newspaper press, partly because it wrongly signaled the death of the book to some nineteenth-century observers and also because I wanted to emphasize certain aspects of print culture that tend to be overlooked at present. Take, for example, the widespread acceptance of Marshall McLuhan's opinion that 'linear, sequential' modes of thought are fostered by printing. This view unaccountably neglects to consider the non-linear, non-sequential format of stories presented in our daily newspapers. Twentieth-century painters experimenting with collage techniques may well have been influenced by the layout of front pages. Exposure to newsprint has probably accustomed successive generations to the juxtaposition of oddly assorted items.

Marshall McLuhan's *Gutenberg Galaxy* justified *its* non-linear presentation with reference to the field theories of modern physics. Given its unconventional format and its substitution of headlines for chapter titles, the influence of the newspaper may be more to the point. Its author's special training not in electromagnetic theory but in English literary studies also needs to be taken into consideration. To be well versed in literary criticism in the 1960s was to be predisposed against historical narratives regardless of other trends. Other anti-historical influences were also at work; Catholic theology, for example. McLuhan's treatment seems to me to owe rather more to St. Augustine than the author was prepared to admit. The sequential approach of the chronicler is, after all, relevant only to the corrupt and time-bound City of Man. The City of God exists outside historical time; all the events that unfold on earth are simultaneously present in the mind of God.

That Catholic theology is not without significance in media analysis is shown not only in the world of McLuhan, who was a Catholic convert, but also in the work of Walter Ong, who is a Jesuit priest. Unlike the Lutherans who hailed printing as God's highest act of grace, Catholic scholars are more likely to remind us that God produced the Incarnation – His truly highest act of grace – in the age of scribes. Thus Ong writes (in *The Presence of the Word*):

God entered human history at the precise time when ... His entrance would have the greatest opportunity to endure and flower.... The believer finds it providential that divine revelation let down roots into human culture ... after the alphabet was devised but before print had overgrown oral structures and before electronic culture had further obscured the basic nature of the word.

(One wonders whether those evangelical preachers who now reach millions of listeners by using the electronic Church would agree that the basic nature of the Word was being obscured.)

For Father Ong, in any event, the age of the scribe was especially privileged for having contained the Incarnation. As already noted, the same age was seen to contain other blessings when the Gothic revival was at its height. Stained glass and illuminated parchments were celebrated even while the colorless and soulless world machine of Enlightenment deists was condemned. The romantic indictment of the age of reason has been preserved intact in McLuhan's *Gutenberg Galaxy: The Making of Typographic Man.* But the arguments that had once been aimed at Voltaire and his followers have been transferred by McLuhan to printing and its effects – with anomalous results. After all, the printed word achieved an unrivaled preeminence when the romantic movement was at its height. How McLuhan's favorite literary artists escaped being contaminated by the all-enveloping effects of typography remains to be explained. Isaac Newton's presumably impoverished single vision is attributed to print culture; whereas William Blake's prophetic imagination is not. Yet surely print played as important a role in the work of the poet and engraver as in that of the mathematical physicist.

As many critics have already noted, the enveloping effects of print are especially apparent in the idiosyncratic formulations of McLuhan himself. He was an omnivorous reader and crammed his text with citations taken from a vast variety of other books. Despite his affinity with nineteenth-century romanticists, he lacked the historical imagination of a Carlyle or a Michelet and made no effort to resurrect the multidimensional rich texture of life as it was lived in the past. Typographic man seems to suffer from the very ailment his creator purports to describe: emerging as an unconvincing and abstract construct assembled by means of scissors and paste.

Scissors and paste are now outmoded; the integrity of the codex is being threatened, and blocks of texts get moved by punching keys. Yet the views held by previous generations cannot be deleted as easily as can words upon a screen. Western attitudes that have survived for so long are likely to persist, no matter how many new electronic instruments are devised. Premature obituaries on the death of the sermon and the end of the book are themselves testimonies to long-enduring habits of mind. In the very act of heralding the dawn of a new age with the advent of new media, contemporary analysts continue to bear witness, however inadvertently, to the ineluctable persistence of the past.

Related Works

Armour, Richard, *The Happy Bookers* (New York, 1976).

Basbanes, Nicholas A., *A Gentle Madness: Bibliophiles, Bibliomanes, and the Eternal Passion for Books* (New York, 1995).

Birkerts, Sven, *The Gutenberg Elegies: The Fate of Reading in an Electronic Age* (Boston and London, 1994).

Blades, William, *The Enemies of Books* (London, 1902).

Brewer, Reginald, *The Delightful Diversion* (New York, 1935).

Brooks, Marshall (ed.), *The Romance of the Book* (Delhi, New York, 1995).

Burns, Eric, *The Joy of Books: Confessions of a Lifelong Reader* (Amherst, New York, 1995).

Carpenter, Kenneth E. (ed.), *Books and Society in History* (New York, 1983).

Cole, John Y. (ed.), *Books in Our Future: Perspectives and Proposals* (Washington, D.C., 1987).

Coover, Robert, 'The End of Books,' in *The New York Times* (21 June 1992).

Davidson, Cathy N. (ed.), *Reading in America* (Baltimore, 1989).

Davies, Robertson, *The Merry Heart: Reflections on Reading, Writing, and The World of Books* (New York and London, 1997).

Denby, David, *Great Books: My Adventures with Homer, Rousseau, Woolf, and Other Indestructible Writers of the Western World* (New York, 1996).

Donaldson, Gerald, *Books: Their History, Art, Power, Glory, Infamy and Suffering According to Their Creators, Friends and Enemies* (New York, 1981).

Dorris, Michael, and Emilie Buchwald (eds), *The Most Wonderful Books: Writers on Discovering the Pleasures of Reading* (Minneapolis, 1997).

Epstein, Joseph, *Plausible Prejudices* (New York, 1985).

——, *One More around the Block* (New York, 1987).

Fadiman, Clifton, *The Reading Lamp* (Cleveland, 1954).

Gilbar, Steven (ed.), *The Book Book* (New York, 1985).

——, *Reading in Bed: Personal Essays on the Glories of Reading* (Boston, 1995).

Iacone, Salvatore J., *The Pleasures of Book Collecting* (New York, 1976).

Illich, Ivan, *In the Vineyard of the Text: A Commentary to Hugh's Didascalicon* (Chicago and London, 1993).

Jennison, Peter S., and Robert N. Sheridan (eds), *The Future of General Adult Books and Reading in America* (Chicago, 1970).

Kernan, Alvin, *The Death of Literature* (New Haven, 1990).

Kertész, André, *On Reading* (New York, 1971).

Korda, Michael, 'The Silver Lining: An Editor Reads for Pleasure,' in *At Random* 14 (1986) 47.

Lee, Charles, *The Hidden Public: The Story of the Book-of-the-Month Club* (Garden City, New York, 1958).

Manguel, Alberto, *A History of Reading* (London, 1996).

Merrill, Christopher, *Your Final Pleasure: An Essay on Reading* (Fredonia, New York, 1996).

Miller, Henry, *The Books in My Life* (New York, 1952).

Miller, J. Hillis, 'Today, Tomorrow: The Intellectual in the Academy and Society,' *PMLA* CXII (1997) 1137–8.

Morrow, Lance, 'The Best Refuge for Insomniacs,' *Time* (29 April 1991).

Moylan, Michele, and Lane Stiles (eds), *Reading Books: Essays on the Material Text and Literature in America* (Amherst, Massachusetts, 1996).

Olmert, Michael, *The Smithsonian Book of Books* (Washington, 1992).

Powell, Lawrence Clark, *A Passion for Books* (Cleveland and New York, 1958).

——, *Books in My Baggage* (Cleveland and New York, 1960).

Proust, Marcel, *On Reading*, trans. by Jean Autret and William Burford (New Haven, 1962).

Raabe, Tom, *Biblioholism: The Literary Addiction* (Golden, Colorado, 1991).

Radway, Janice A., *A Feeling for Books: The Book-of-the-Month Club, Literary Taste, and Middle-Class Desire* (Chapel Hill and London, 1997).

Raphael, Fredric (ed.), *Bookmarks* (London, 1975).

Rostenberg, Leona and Madeleine Stern, *Old Books, Rare Friends: Two Literary Sleuths and Their Shared Passion* (New York and London, 1997).

Schwartz, Lynne Sharon, *Ruined by Reading: A Life in Books* (Boston, 1996).

Toth, Susan Allen, and John Coughlan (eds), *Reading Rooms* (New York and London, 1991).

Welty, Eudora, *One Writer's Beginnings* (Cambridge, Massachusetts and London, 1984).

Woolf, Virginia, 'How Should One Read a Book?', in *The Common Reader*, second series (London, 1932).

Index